Natalie = Found =
"Up North" and
thought of you!

Love,
Aunt Kristine

Fishing & Hunting By Canoe

by Bob Cary

Author: Bob Cary

Editor: Anne Swenson
Layout & Design: Nick Wognum

Published by
Singing River Publications, Inc.
PO Box 72
Ely, MN 55731-0072
www.singingriverpublications.com

ISBN: 0-9774831-1-8

Printed in Canada.

DEDICATION

Many key people were involved with the compiling, editing and publishing of this book. First, credit must go to my wife Edith who provides a quiet, comfortable atmosphere in which to work and was the bow paddler in many of our fishing and canoe camping trips.

Nick Wognum, general manager of the Ely Echo Newspaper, set the type, laid out the pages and illustrations. Anne Swenson, publisher of the Ely Echo Newspaper, where I have worked for over 30 years, has been a patient and valuable editor of my columns. Chris Moroni, the publisher of this book, gave support and offered valuable suggestions as to its format and content.

Some of the material in this book has been rewritten from my previous book "The Big Wilderness Canoe Manual," which was compiled in 1978 at the behest of Chet Fish, a former editor of Outdoor Life. Much of it is new. All of it has been fun to write, illustrate and assemble.

Foreword

The canoe, as originated by the American Indian, was a craft uniquely designed for fishing and hunting. At times it was used for gathering, travel and war, but its chief purposes were for acquiring fish and game, staples in the diet of the Ojibwe, Cree, Micmac, Abnaki, Malecite, Ottawa, Huron, Algonquin, Winnebago and other people located on the North American waterways. It is a craft used extensively for those same purposes by people of North America today.

Historians may say what they want about the impact of European explorers and settlers on the native people of the canoe country, but the native people also had an impact on the newcomers. Immigrants were very quick to understand the utility of the canoe and adopt it for their own use. Its design has changed little over the centuries; only the materials have changed.

There are still birch bark canoes being made. Some of us have owned and used such craft. Today they are considered more as collector's items or as pieces of art than as water vehicles; but their descendants, made of wood, canvas, aluminum, fiber glass, Kevlar and various other durable and lightweight materials are still considered unmatched for certain types of water-related fishing and hunting.

However, as the general population of North America expanded and more people became acquainted with canoes, much of its emphasis changed to recreational paddling, canoe camping and racing. Many who fish and hunt by canoe may also engage in those other activities, but the main focus is still to harvest fish and game. In these pursuits, over many decades, canoe anglers and hunters have acquired some perceptions and skills unique to their pursuits, not usually described in books or magazines devoted to canoeing. Perceptions include hull designs which lend themselves best to such pursuits. Skills include the ability to engage in such activity in rain, sleet, snow and howling wind and yet remain upright and dry.

Let the author hasten to point out that little, if any, of the material encompassed in this book was his own invention or discovery. In 80 years of canoe travel, every useful concept was acquired from others- guides, American Indians, professional anglers, outfitters, trappers, hunters- outdoor folk who fished and hunted, some for their livelihood, some for recreation.

It could be said that these outdoor folk comprise the finest and most honorable group of citizens one could hope to meet, but it wouldn't be true. A lot of them were indeed very fine, honorable and upstanding citizens; but some of them were poachers, thieves, eminently immoral and often drunks to boot, but they had canoe skills worth adopting. As in all human enterprises, you take the best and discard the rest.

As our Ojibwe neighbors say: "Min-ooh way-way-bah-nah-bi; min-ooh gie-we-say, nee-gee."

"Good fishing and good hunting, friend!

Fishing & Hunting By Canoe

Chapter I
A MATTER OF STEALTH

The canoe-borne fisherman or hunter, moving over the water surface soundlessly, is less an intruder than a part of the natural order. He or she becomes absorbed into the natural environment like nature's other water-related fishers or hunters such as the otter, marten, mink, loon, heron, eagle or osprey.

A canoe in the hands of a skilled and knowledgeable paddler is the most efficient water-oriented means for humans to slip up upon unsuspecting fish or game. First is the essential silence. In experienced hands, a canoe can be propelled with no more water disturbance than the ripple of an otter. The close proximity of the fisherman with the water environment allows for continual observation of the habitat of the species pursued. Information stored in the canoe angler's cranial computer allows him to assess even new waters with a somewhat high expectation of success.

When stalking game, the hunter, sitting or kneeling motionless, can drift or effortlessly scull his craft within range of his target. The American Indian tribes of northern waters were masters of silent

1

canoe travel, moving effortlessly along stream and lakeshore.

Certainly, the native paddlers had extra reasons for such stealth. The various tribes were often in conflict with one another. Any enemy detecting movement was apt to stalk a careless hunter or hurry ahead and prepare an ambush, such as befell the legendary John Tanner on the Maligne River. Thus the hunter could become the hunted.

Early voyageurs and frontiersmen, passing through hostile territory, exhibited considerable caution or suffered the consequences. Today's outdoorsman or outdoorswoman operates with similar caution, not necessarily from the standpoint of avoiding ambush, but simply to get undetected within range of whatever targets are selected.

With the increased popularity of canoes, a large amount of emphasis has been devoted to craft designed specifically for recreational paddling, camping and racing. These pursuits often lend themselves to narrow, sleek lines and extreme light weight. Inevitably, a vast amount of written lore has been produced and consumed involving paddle craft. Indeed, volumes. Nearly all of these sources tout lightness and speed of travel. A few books devote perhaps a chapter or so to the harvest of fish and, more rarely, game as somewhat of as afterthought. There are some elements of the paddle gentry who abhor the taking of game and thus many authors skirt the issue entirely, preferring to pretend it does not occur, although all canoe writers recognize that the native designers of our craft certainly spent a significant portion of their time in search of meat. Thus most of the current canoe literature, while accurate, is slanted toward lightweight, fast paddling designs and may or may not be relevant to the paddle pushing angler and hunter.

Indian canoes, on the other hand, were essentially fishing and

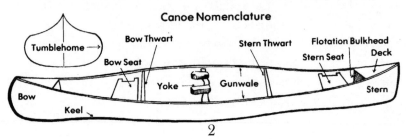

Canoe Nomenclature

hunting craft with ample beam, adequate rocker and tumblehome. Most were easy to maneuver, had good stability, could safely accommodate a good load even in a stiff wind and had adequate freeboard. By many of today's standards they were heavy and slow, but they were admirably suited to the purposes of native fishermen and hunters. And many of these design characteristics are still quite valid for those of us who use canoes mainly to fish and shoot. We are sharply aware that it is not advisable to attempt moving a couple of buck deer or a two quarters of a bull moose in a 38 pound, narrow racing hull.

The North American Indians designed bark canoes in a variety of shapes and sizes, all built for specific uses and conditions. There was no attempt to create the "perfect" canoe if there ever was such a thing. They were built to perform certain functions.

No question but what there are canoes being made these days which are extremely fast. If speed is what is sought. Some eminent authorities, from time to time, are apt point out that today's paddle craft are infinitely lighter and faster than anything the native builders could have imagined. The inference is that the old time canoe builders had limited knowledge and we are a darn sight smarter. A rather tenuous belief.

Those of us who grew up in the 1920s were acquainted with

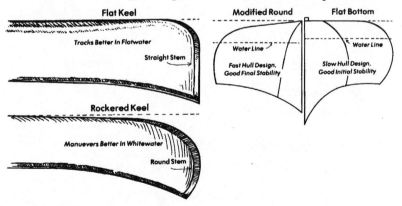

canoes which were extremely stable. I was brought up in a wide, stable 18-foot Old Town wood-and-canvas Guide Model, a heavy vessel which weighed around 90 pounds dry, a hundred wet. We commonly fly fished from this craft (there was no such thing as spin fishing in those days) with one paddler handling the canoe from the stern and the fisherman casting while standing in the bow.

Standing? Absolutely. For many years I fished with an expert flyrodder named Roy Nord who learned his skills on the trout rivers of Michigan's Upper Peninsula. Roy positioned himself sideways with one leg braced against the bow seat, the other farther toward the bow. Casting was accomplished across beam so that the backcast did not jab a barb in the ear of the stern paddler. Periodically, we would switch with Roy handling the paddle while I took my turn casting from the bow. All canoe anglers did it that way and it required only ordinary dexterity.

When a fish was on, the bow angler immediately sat down, lowering the center of gravity until our tiring quarry was brought to the surface near the stern paddler who also wielded the landing net. One would need acrobatic skills, not to mention considerable luck, to attempt laying out a fly or cork popper while standing up in many of our current craft. Beam and stability have been sacrificed for lightness and speed. And many modern hulls are nearly impossible to maneuver in any sort of a cross wind although most anglers are aware that fish tend to feed mainly on the windward shore rather than in the lee.

There are still hulls being made which are designed for fishing

Homemade Oak Yoke

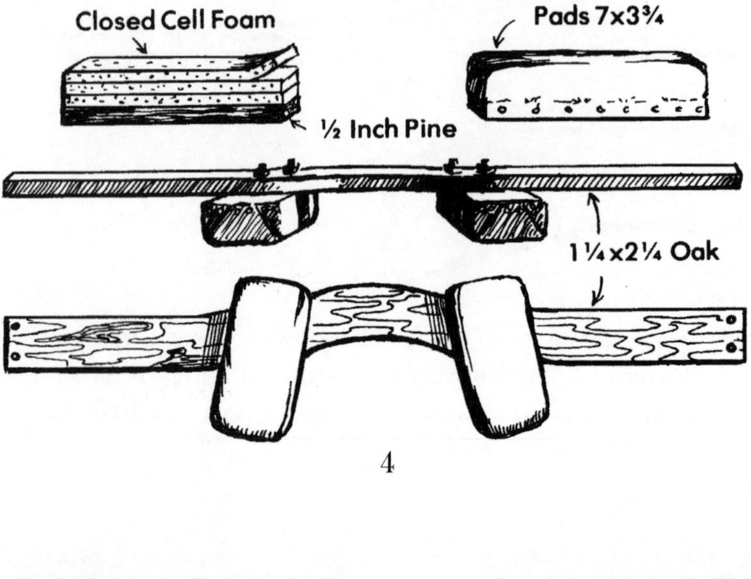

Closed Cell Foam

Pads 7x3¾

½ Inch Pine

1¼x2¼ Oak

and hunting or which lend themselves to those pursuits. While the racers and recreational paddle campers have run off with the game, most canoe makers have understandably followed the trend, tending to go where the most money is. The serious canoe angler and shooter not only needs to look around and compare various hulls, but also should try them out.

Furthermore, some of today's craft are simply impossible to hunt from. The canoe of grandpa's day had high woven cane seats which facilitated shooting - jump shooting ducks in a wild rice marsh or stalking deer or moose. While the stern paddler controlled the craft, the bow man did the shooting. To accomplish this with some degree of comfort and accuracy, he positioned himself sideways on the seat. If he was right handed, his right shoulder was back to cradle the gun stock against his cheek, left leg extended toward the bow, right leg tucked under the seat. For accuracy, either shotgun or rifle shooting was done across the body, not face -on.

The huntability of any modern, low seat, narrow hull can be tested without even getting on the water. Simply prop up the fast, low-profile, bucket-seat canoe in the yard and step inside with an empty gun. Slide onto the front seat and settle in with both feet forward (there is no other place to put them). Assume a target has appeared directly off the bow. Raise the weapon, which will come up facing directly forward, a near impossible position from which to shoot. The bucket seat has the shooter's rear end anchored in such a way he cannot swing his body sideways and there is no room under the low seat to tuck his right leg. It is hardly possible to aim and shoot from this position, much less with any measure of accuracy.

OK. So that eliminates a lot of hulls if hunting is contemplated. What to look for then? Ideally, the craft should have plenty of beam for stability, a flat bow seat on which the shooter's rear end can be swiveled around (woven cane seats work fine.) The seat must be of sufficient height from the floor to get the right leg bent underneath and there should be bow room to accommodate the left leg.

The importance of stability cannot be over emphasized in shooting. There is considerable recoil from, say, a 12 gauge duck gun if fired off the beam. The canoe is apt to rock. If a flock of ducks is escaping off one side of the craft and both hunters fire at the same time, there is a real possibility of overturning. Add the accompanied lurching and shifting of a 90-pound Labrador retriever and the swamping odds go up sharply. With a narrow, round hull, a shooter is quite likely to wind up in the water, gun and all. No question but what a veteran stern paddler, skillful and alert, is a valuable asset to stability and may many times avert disaster. The stern man will react automatically with an extended paddle brace on the side opposite the direction of the shot to absorb recoil and offset any tendency of the canoe to roll. But if the paddler and bow gunner both shoot, look out!

Usually, it takes only an experience or two with a narrow, low-gunwale, low-seat, straight-keeled, non-rockered hull for the angler or shooter to discover the drawbacks. The problem is finding a hull which will do the job.

Old Town still makes paddle craft for hunters and anglers. But so do others. There are a number of small builders around the country, men like Ely's Joe Seliga, who became canoe-building legends for not compromising their designs to the modem obsession with speed. Some of the historic wood-and-canvas canoes designed for angling and shooting included Faber and White, now collector's items.

Back in 1945, when World War II came to an end, the Grumman Company found itself with a large supply of aluminum and no more market for fighter planes. Grumman began turning out aluminum canoes with traditional hunting and fishing hulls. For four decades two of our favorite craft were a 15-foot lightweight (55 pound) Grumman and an 18-foot lightweight (67 pound) Grumman. Both of these craft had a lot of initial stability, high, flat seats, were not too heavy and were easy to keep clean. Their only drawback in hunting was the fact that one had to be careful not to hit the metal gunwale with a gun or a paddle because it would boom like a base drum and scare any wildlife nearby.

Alumacraft produced excellent paddle craft for fishing and hunt-

6

ing with a somewhat sharper bow than the Grumman, yet retaining a wide, flat bottom for stability along with high, flat seats. Many sportsmen believe the Alumacraft design provides the fastest metal hull along with durability and low maintenance. A lot of outdoor folk swear by Alumacraft canoes and thousands are in service today handling multiple angling and shooting chores.

We have used a number of modern, very light Kevlar craft for fishing and hunting, some of which were adequate with seat modifications. Currently, we are using both a 16-foot and 18.5 foot Kevlar craft. These hulls are extremely light, have adequate width and stability and are designed with moderate rocker which allows for maneuverability. We have modified our personal craft by raising the flat cane seats two inches providing more leg room for angling and shooting.

There are good hulls on the market and it pays the angler and hunter to shop around. Most canoe dealers will allow a trial run with a canoe. There is nothing like getting the craft in the water before buying to see how it handles for fishing or shooting. And the test should include use of fishing gear. A canoe answers a lot of questions if the bow paddler is wielding a rod and reel. If the buyer is also a shooter, the canoe should be tested with a firearm aboard. Duck hunters can try out their craft using a hand trap to hurl clay pigeons across the water. A rifleman can test the stability of his craft by drifting along and firing a couple of rounds at a target on shore straight off the bow and a couple off the beam. Let it be made plain that there is nothing wrong with low, narrow, round hulls with bucket seats for fast cruising or occasional racing. It is just that fishing and hunting are a lot more fun with hulls designed more for those uses.

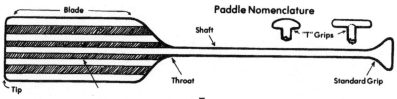

7

Chapter 2
BACK PADDLING

The handiest maneuver, indeed an essential one for serious canoe angling, is the reverse scull or back paddle. The stern paddler
grips the paddle shaft with one hand on the paddle throat, locks
the shaft against his arm behind his elbow and keeps the blade in
the water. This allows him to control the speed and direction of
the craft traveling backward by a sculling movement of the blade.
He can scull straight back, or to one side or the other as necessary.

This is strictly for fishing, not for traveling. To get quickly from
fishing spot to fishing spot, there is no substitute for traditional
straight forward paddling. But when fishermen want to keep a canoe in one position, or edge it along slowly up-current or upwind,
sculling backward is key.

In addition, this allows the stern paddler a free arm with which
to fish. Canoe guides use this method continually, sculling the craft
around so the client in the bow is kept within easy casting distance
of the shoreline or is being drifted over underwater structure. At
the same time, the guide usually has a line over the side with which,
one-handed, he can manipulate a jig or live bait. With a fish on, he
simply lays the paddle across the center thwart and goes about his

business with a both hands..

If there is any kind of wind or current present, it is difficult for the stern paddler to control the craft by paddling in a traditionally forward manner. With the bow angler simply fishing instead of paddling, the canoe will waver off course, become unmanageable and blow over the preferred fishing spot. In dead still water, the canoe can be managed a number of ways, but in a breeze or a current, the reverse scull is required.

This is particularly effective when using live bait such as minnows, worms or leeches. Back paddling allows the canoe to be moved at whatever speed is deemed necessary and in a direction to carry the bait along a break line, weed line or around submerged reefs or sunken trees. Some anglers, using electronic devices, continually study their screen and when spotting fish below, will slow down their backward movement, perhaps hover over the fish while their baits are probing the structure.

Back paddling is not particularly effective as a trolling method simply because it takes too much effort to keep the canoe moving at trolling speed. Trolling is usually done best moving forward with both anglers paddling if necessary. There is no real need for either angler to hold onto his rod. More on this in the chapter titled "Canoe Trolling."

Canoe guides not only scull from the stern, but also control just about all other activities including handling the anchor, parceling out live bait, and netting fish. Two experienced fishing buddies or a veteran husband-wife team, may divide the effort. This is covered in the chapter "Bow Angler."

Guides prefer controlling activity from the stern seat where they can keep an eye on whatever is happening. If their client gets snagged on an underwater obstruction, the guide can ease over or past it and have the bow angler bounce the rod tip up and down

9

until the hook is freed. If it won't come free and the line needs to be hauled on with effort, the canoe can be paddled over and past the snag, causing the bow angler's line to swing back where the line can be gripped by the guide and reefed until it pops loose or the line is broken. The guide does this rather than have the client in the bow flail around and possibly swamp the craft.

Fishing in thick submerged timber, some guides have a couple of devices to work hooks loose. Years ago on a log-filled flowage, I fished with Wisconsin walleye specialist Chet Quillen, who carried a 14-foot cane pole sticking out of the back of the watercraft. At the tip of the pole was taped a screw eye, the eye bent open. When hung up, which was often, he would slide the screw eye down the line with the cane pole until he hit the lure, then shoved it off the log with a hefty push. Some fishermen use an extra lead-weighted line with a hook on the lead weight which can be slid down the line and the weight bounced up and down until the lure comes free.

In a stream, the back-paddle is useful in controlling downstream movement. This allows the stern paddler to not only determine direction, but also speed, back paddling when wishing to hold the craft above a certain eddy or pool, allowing it to drift forward when moving ahead.

Once anglers master the sculling technique, they usually find their success rate improves sharply.

Chapter 3
LANDING FISH

One of the quickest ways to get intimate with the aquatic environment is to commit an error when landing a fish. Some of us have done it. Nearly all of us have seen it done. Usually it involves a big fish, a trophy, a monster. Something we fiercely desire to capture, if for no more than a photo op. Bragging material.

However, anyone who doesn't get excited connecting with a monstrous bass, trout, walleye or pike should probably quit fishing. I've been at this for 80 years and still the sight of a huge, silvery rainbow trout, a jut-jawed, six-pound smallmouth bass, a marble-eyed 30-inch walleye or a four-foot pike give me a pounding heart, shortness of breath and shaky hands. It also warns me, from past experience, that disaster could be imminent.

Most of the problems associated with hooking into a trophy fish involve an immediate and compulsive desire to land it. Right now. Which is where most possible troubles may originate. No big fish should be rushed. Not only from the standpoint of successfully coping with the trophy, but also considering one's safety. If it is possible to calmly follow accepted procedure (not always attain-

11

able), the fish may be played until it is worn to a frazzle and wobbling on the surface, which makes step two easier: getting it into the canoe. The problem is, once the leviathan comes into view, capturing it often becomes a matter of haste.

Probably the hairiest north country fish to land in a canoe is a giant pike or muskie. Any member of the pike family is a problem because it is long, slippery with slime and has a mouth full of needle-sharp teeth. Most canoe guides carry landing nets. A few carry one of those nets with a folding handle. The nets we use are relatively small, trout stream size, will slip inside a packsack for traveling and portaging, but hardly having the capacity to land more than a third of a big pike.

What then? An ordinary cotton work glove is a handy accessory, not only for big pike but for landing other species. The glove makes it possible to grip a slippery fish and create some control over its expected thrashing about when lifted from the water. We carry a left-handed glove which can be slipped on in emergency (the right hand is gripping the fishing rod). After use, the glove may be rinsed out in the water, wrung out, dried, then stuck in the packsack or in a pocket. The glove will work adequately for most fish, including pike up to 12 pounds or so. For real honkers, 15 to 25 pounds, the safest procedure is to beach them.

Most canoe anglers do not anticipate socking into a scissor-jaw of 20 pounds or more; but it can easily occur and the furor generated is often entertaining to behold. A fish that big can create an impressive, foam-splattered performance with powerful runs and some surface-shattering leaps. No matter that this denizen of the deep is far too large for any thought of eating, the immediate attempt is to land it at all costs.

Over a few decades of experience, we have determined the safest move is to locate a shallow sand bar or sloping granite ledge where the fish can be captured, photographed, unhooked and released. Initially, the hooked fish needs to be directed away from weed thickets or submerged timber and carefully played out until it is more amenable to capture. In the canoe country, most shores are steep, rocky and brush-strewn; but one occasionally finds a sand beach or a gently-sloping granite ledge where the activity may be terminated. Once the tired fish begins to roll on the surface, it can be gently towed to shore. It pays to scan the landing site for sharp rocks or sunken tree branches which could foil the attempted landing. Give a big fish anything to wrap around and it will. One lunge and it is all over. The fish is not only free, but free with possibly $6 worth of artificial lure in his mouth.

If we find a hazard-free, gently-sloping sand shore or ledge, the canoe can be beached where the angler may step out while keeping a tight line on the wallowing prize. The next move is to coax the big fish gently toward shore, recognizing that the moment its belly hits solid bottom, it will tear off in at least one more slashing run. With that burst of defiance out of the way, the fish can be edged inshore where the rod may be laid down and the trophy safety lifted up with both hands. In the meantime, the companion has secured the canoe, laid his paddle down and has the camera out of the pack for several quick shots. Then the giant may be unhooked, eased toward deep water and saluted as it swims off. Once upon a time, anglers would attempt to keep such trophies alive as long as possible, then rush them to civilization with the hope of a mount at a taxidermy shop. This is still possible, but current procedure is to quickly measure the fish and release it.

Measurements taken of length and girth allows a taxidermist to convert the dimensions to a lifelike graphite mount which permits the angler to have his wall trophy without killing the fish. Length may be marked on a canoe paddle or fish pole and a piece of fish line used to measure the girth.

Bass are much easier to land and most will fit in even a small landing net. It is also possible to land them with a canvas glove or simply reach down, place the thumb inside the fish's mouth, a forefinger under its jaw and lift. The bass will come up with scarcely a wiggle. It may be held thus, hoisted to eye level or otherwise displayed for a quick photo and release. Speed is essential if the intent is to release the fish with a minimum of harm and stress.

Walleyes present a unique challenge because they have razor-sharp gill covers that can inflict serious damage on one's hand if gripped wrongly. A net is handy, so is the canvas glove. If the fish is being landed bare-handed, the safest way is to grip it from the underside of the gills, keeping the palm and fingers away from those gill covers. Shoot the photo; put it back. A few walleyes to be processed for dinner can be impaled on a stringer and kept alive until supper time. Tastiest walleyes for this endeavor are those about 13 to 15 inches. Occasionally, we keep larger walleyes for baking.

Big trout are very slippery and present a problem, perhaps best solved with a landing net or by simply bringing the played-out trophy alongside the canoe where the hook may be slipped out backward without even touching the fish. If soundly hooked, it may be possible to release it with needle-nosed pliers. Because trout are exceedingly slippery, they can be damaged by gripping them too tight. Keeping them out of the water too long while unhooking them can be lethal. In warm weather it is imperative to get big trout unhooked and released quickly because they are often brought up from deep, cold water to the warm surface and suffer shock. Smaller trout, which are being kept to eat, are best stored in a wet cotton bag like an old pillow slip. The wet cloth will keep the fish cool and fresh. Trout placed on a stringer will go soft and become unfit for eating. Some of us gill and gut our trout the moment we catch them, an added enhancement to the flavor.

When fishing with live bait and a big fish is hooked too deep to remove the hook without damage, we simply clip the line and free it. A hook stuck in a fish's neck will "rust out" within a period of time with no permanent injury to the fish. We know this because over the years we have captured a number of fish still carrying someone else's hook, fish which had managed to break the line and get away. They do not seem overly encumbered by a hook or lure stuck in their jaws. Indeed, several times we have had a large pike on the hook which broke free and sometime later in the day we hooked and landed that same fish with the original lure still in its jaw.

One of the worst situations which can develop with extra large fish is to get it inside the hull of the canoe before it is thoroughly

14

tired. Pike, particularly, are notorious for not putting up a spectacular initial battle and may sometimes be brought into the canoe still full of fight. At this point it will begin a thrashing, smashing series of acrobatics, knocking over tackle boxes and possibly getting hooks tangled up in packs, pants or even a human epidermis. When possible, it is usually best not to bring big fish on board. Keep them in the water where they can be netted, gloved or otherwise dealt with. Most really big ones can be released with the assistance of long-nosed pliers using a flick of the wrist.

In any case, the person with the fish on the line should handle that situation. The other canoeist needs to be alert, paddle ready to maneuver the canoe and perhaps extend a paddle brace in the event that his companion gets overly-excited at the big fish and does something silly like shift his weight to the side of the canoe. There are many instances where an angler attempting to land a fish, leaned out too far from the gunwale and swamped the craft. This can be a great source of hilarity if one is observing the activity from another canoe. If one is in the canoe when it goes over, the humor is seldom readily apparent.

Chapter 4
TROLLING

The boat angler, used to trolling by outboard with the movement controlled by the motor which allows him to sit relaxed, rod-in-hand, needs to learn some new skills for a paddle canoe. Two of these involve controlling direction and maintaining correct speed. In a mild wind or gentle current, the stern paddler can usually control both; but in a stiff breeze or swift current, it may require both paddlers to keep the craft on course, prevent it from getting sideways or crashing into the shore.

The first problem with canoe trolling is what to do with the fishing rods. Obviously, neither angler can propel the craft forward while holding the rod in either hand. Some stern anglers will set the drag on the reel and lay the rod alongside one leg, tip aimed off the stern. This maneuver results in a direct connection to the reel if a fish strikes. If it is a big fish and the drag set tight, the rod and reel may suddenly leap up and vanish off the stern. This may sound improbable, but all of us have seen it happen. It is best to have the rod situated so the tip projects 90 degrees to the side, allowing some bend in the rod when a fish strikes. This also allows some cushion for the drag to release.

Certainly, when a strike occurs on a trolled lure, the hooks need be set quickly or the fish may be lost. This means the rod must be easily reached and free for the hook to be set. Some anglers use metal rod holders, clamped to the canoe gunwale. We don't like any encumbrance on the gunwales in case we need to do some quick recovery strokes. Thus, we anchor our rods with our knees.

Assuming most anglers are right-handed, most paddling will be done from the right side. The rod, of necessity, must be aimed out the left. We lay the rod over the gunwale ahead of and tight against the left knee cap. The handle of the rod is shoved in behind the right knee, the edge of the butt resting on the right gunwale. This may sound nuts, but in actual use, the rod is securely anchored and easily reached. With a strike, the left hand grabs the rod and sets the hook while the right hand lays the paddle down. The rod is switched to the right hand and the left hand slides down to grip the reel handle. The battle is on! This system can be used on the right side of the canoe if paddling is being done on the left. The bow paddler has his rod out the side opposite the stern paddler to prevent tangles and to maintain paddle coordination.

Unlike in a power boat where the bow passenger can simply sit and enjoy the scenery, the bow paddler in a canoe has his own job when trolling. One is to paddle lightly but steadily to offset wind or current. Another is be alert in the event the stern angler gets a strike and needs to drop his paddle to play the fish. The bow paddler can keep the canoe headed upwind or up-current, into open water and away from shoreline structure. The bow paddler then controls the craft while the stern angler lands his fish.

It is good form for the bow man to have his paddle handy at all times, anyway, in case a sudden gust of wind whips the canoe off course and a few extra strokes from the front would get the craft back in direction. Experienced canoe anglers know this and nobody has to say: "Hey, grab your paddle and help me out." The bow man simply does it. Also, if the stern angler ties into a real trophy, it may be necessary for the bow man to get the canoe out into deep water. Since much of the activity is occurring behind the bow man's back, largely out of his vision, he needs to develop a sixth sense in what is needed so he can react automatically in such situations without having to swivel around and study the problem. One advantage of paddle trolling is that the canoe can be immediately stopped if the lure snags up. It takes but a moment to back paddle to the snag and pop the hook loose. In the event both anglers get a fish on at the same time, about all that can be done is to keep tight lines and paddle one-handed to a distance offshore where one fish can be landed, then the other. In a stiff wind, this can be a mess and it may be that one angler simply breaks his fish off so he can handle the canoe for his partner or allow his line to run free and hope the fish stays on the hook.

When trolling with live bait, which requires the fish to "run" after a strike, the drag may be set extra light. This will allow the fish to take off with the bait; but the angler will see by the bending of his rod tip that a fish in on. He can re-set the drag with one hand when he picks up the rod. Some anglers are quick enough to reach down and flip the bail free so the fish can run with the bait. We use whatever seems to work at the time.

Sometimes, when trout are active, we troll streamer flies or tiny lures on our flyrods.

Most of this action takes place in smaller lakes where wind is less of a problem and the bow angler can simply hang onto his tackle, rod tip aimed back and off to one side. Indeed, sometimes the bow angler may find it convenient to sits backward, facing the stern paddler.

The stern flyrod troller has a larger problem, paddling and fishing at the same time. He cannot very easily anchor the rod against his knee as with spin tackle. We have had a measure of success by laying the flyrod handle and reel across the center thwart, with the rod balanced where it rests on the gunwale, tip aimed to the stern. If the rod is angled out slightly to the side, there is a measure of immediate "spring" with a strike and then the reel will release line, allowing the hooked fish to run. This is recognizably not a good way to operate, but it allows a fair number of strikes to be hooked and we have boated some nice rainbows and brookies from small lakes in this manner. We have also, unfortunately, lost a number of pricey streamers and lures.

18

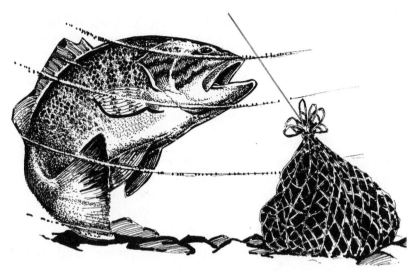

Chapter Five
USING AN ANCHOR

Because canoes are light and have considerable length, they are subject to being manipulated by wind and current. There is not much that is more aggravating than getting the craft located on a school of fish and then have it blown or swept out of casting range. And it can happen in the flick of an eyelash.

Using some sort of an anchor to hold the craft in one spot, frees up both anglers to do some serious fishing. There are a number of lightweight metal anchors on the market designed especially for canoe work. All are serviceable, but some are bulky, have sharp metal angles or points and are unhandy for carrying in packs. Some canoe men simply carry an extra 50-foot section of 1/8-inch nylon line which is tied to a rock of suitable weight and shape, picked up along shore. When portaging, the rock is discarded and a new one selected as needed. Another workable system is to use a nylon mesh bag, like the net in a basketball hoop. The bottom of the net is tied shut and a line threaded through the top making a closure which can be pulled shut after the net is filled with rocks for weight. The bag is secured to the anchor line. When done fishing or making a portage, the rocks are dumped out, the empty bag rolled up and stuffed in the pack.

All anglers know that fish tend to feed on the windward shore or on top of reefs where the waves are breaking in. This is a situation which sometimes difficult to handle from canoe unless the anchor line is fastened to the bow. Some canoes are built with a drilled and grommeted bow hole, some with a metal bow loop to which the anchor line can be lashed. Our preference is to run a four-foot section of nylon line through the bow hole and tie it to form a loop. The anchor line is fed through this loop so the anchor can be let down to the proper depth and the line cinched to the loop, holding the canoe in place. With the canoe anchored nose into the wind, it will ride the waves smoothly and evenly. When the anglers want to move, the bow paddler leans over, pulls in the bow loop until he reaches the anchor line, unties it and pulls the anchor back into the canoe.

Where the wind is moderate, an anchor may be lashed off one side, but this may result in the canoe seesawing back and forth. If the wind rises, there is a chance that the canoe could swamp.

For stream fishing, we know some anglers who prefer a section of heavy chain, one end tied to the anchor line which is let out over the stern. The chain is dragged straight off the stern to keep the craft parallel with the current. By adjusting the length of the anchor line, the drag can be increased or lessened to control speed downstream. The advantage of the chain is simply that it never seems to get hung up on underwater snags so the anglers never have to paddle back upstream to get their anchor loose.

Any time a canoe is anchored in a strong wind, care must be taken to make sure waves can't come in over the side. It is good practice to tie the anchor line with a quick release hitch, one which can be freed simply by yanking on a loose end. In the event of any emergency, the anchor line can be released allowing the canoe anglers the freedom to handle their craft. In the event (heaven forbid) that the canoe swamps, a quick release hitch allows the anchor line to be immediately freed so the canoe can be towed to shore.

One other thing: Canoe lines can cause trouble. One of these is getting a fish wrapped around it which will necessitate pulling in the anchor to get the hook and/or fish loose. The other is the loose coil of anchor rope lying in a pile inside at the canoe hull, waiting to get tangled up in lures, feet, stringer, you name it. With the anchor situated upwind off the bow, there is much less chance of getting the fish tangled in the rope. And if the angler keeps the excess anchor line neatly coiled and under the seat, it is less apt to get snarled with other items.

It is good practice when raising the anchor, to simply reach out and lift with the arms. It is not safe to lean the body out over the gunwale and lift because this invites the chance that the anchor will stick, the angler lose his balance and fall in or cause the canoe to tip over.

Anchors are essential when serious fishing is involved. The canoe can be positioned upwind, off a choice reef and held there while both anglers cast. When a fish is hooked, it can be played and brought to net without having the canoe blow inshore or away from the fishing spot. When bait fishing or vertical jigging, if a school of fish is located deep off the side of a structure, the canoe can be moved slightly upwind, the anchor dropped and the line let out until the fishermen are directly over the target area.

When stream fishing some canoemen use a section of heavy chain for an anchor. The chain is hung out the stern on six feet or more of quarter inch nylon rope. The chain has the advantage of dragging on the bottom and slowing down the downstream progress without hanging up on rocks or logs and the speed of the drift can be controlled by the amount of rope let out.

When "lining" a canoe up a set of rapids we would rather not portage around, we use about fifty feet of rope, tied to the bow and to the center thwart, forming a triangle. One canoeman walking up the shore, holding onto the center of the rope triangle can guide the craft upstream through considerable current.. By lengthening or shortening the lines, the bow angle can be adjusted so the canoe can be led against the current without much effort.

Chapter Six

FISHING THREE OR MORE

Suggesting that three or more people can fish comfortably from a canoe sometimes causes purists to recoil in horror. However, it goes on all the time. Canoe guides often take two guests with them in the same craft. Families regularly fish three to a canoe - in some instances, where youngsters are involved, four may be in the same canoe. In the chapter on paddling, the method of three driving a canoe is covered. Fishing has a somewhat similar seating arrangement, but more care need be taken to keep hooks out of clothing or various parts of the epidermis.

Some canoes, in 18 or 18.5 length, are built with three seats, designed specifically by the manufacturer to balance and paddle easily with an extra passenger. There are also canoe seat inserts which lock over the gunwales. Some guides like both clients forward of the center thwart, one in the bow seat, one just ahead of the center. Others find it handier to have the third person positioned just behind the center thwart, figuring he is less apt to get tangled up with the bow angler. The problem with the third person behind the center thwart is that it puts that person just ahead of the stern paddler's knees, which puts the rear paddler in continual danger of a hook in the head. In any case, the guide or stern paddler usually just handles the craft and does little fishing unless drifting with live bait.

It is enough to have the bow and center anglers casting lures and it takes just about the full attention for the stern paddler to keep the canoe parallel to the shore and within easy casting distance. Also, if fishing is good and both front anglers connect at the same time, it is quite enough work for the stern paddler to handle the canoe and land the fish. Having three fish on at once is total bedlam.

It is imperative that both the bow and middle angler cast in the same direction, preferably off the left side of the canoe so both lures go out parallel and don't get crossed. Also, by casting off the left side of the canoe, both angler's overhead casts are in an arc safely up and away from the stern paddler's head.

With three experienced anglers, chores can be divided up. The bow angler is in a good position to handle the anchor. The center fisherman can be put in charge of the bait if live bait is being used. The stern paddler is probably in the best position to net fish and put them on the stringer. In any event, a stringer trailing off the stern creates less of a steering problem than one tied amidships.

Two parents with two kids in a canoe can accommodate four lines by fishing straight down with live bait. No way in creation would my wife and I consider having two kids casting from the center of the canoe. Fishing with live bait over the side works well by drifting the craft over sunken reefs or along weed lines. If there is even a slight breeze, an anchor may be necessary. The anchored canoe gives both bow and stern adults two free hands to deal with bait, hooks, landing fish or any problems arising from the kids in the center.

One thing about kids, they sometimes have a short attention span. If the fish aren't biting, they may lose interest. A cooler with

23

cold pop, a thermos with cold lemonade, a few extra candy bars or chips are helpful in maintaining interest. If the fish don't bite in one spot, keep moving, paddling up the shore, nosing into stream mouths, inspecting beaver houses, looking for eagle nests, perhaps even getting out of the canoe to stretch legs, hike a trail, pick wild berries or check out campsites.

Grandparents are particularly good at this. Grandparents have a special relationship with kids because they usually have charge of them at fun times. Grandparents are more tolerant and don't expect a whole lot. If a kid gets a horrendous tangle in his line, grandpa or grandma will patiently help straighten out the mess with humor and without a lecture. Grandparents are usually full of sympathy if a fish breaks the line or gets away. Parents criticize. Parents lecture. Grandparents sympathize. Grandparents praise.

Also, grandparents get very excited over whatever the kids catch, even if it is no more than a little perch or sunfish. Anything with scales and fins is a trophy and can be the source of a brief discussion about the species and its position in the natural scheme of things. Kids are fascinated with nature and are very impressed if the adults can describe life histories of fish along with identifying birds and animals along shore.

Early morning and late evening are excellent times to cruise silently along shorelines and into bays with the possibility of viewing beavers at work, herons fishing, a family of otters whopping down a mud slide or even - moose in the water up to his knees. A fishing expedition can be more noteworthy for kids if the adults are not simply focused on filling a stringer. However, filling a stringer has its own rewards, especially if it is followed by filleting and frying the catch. It is never too early to instruct a youngster in the process of rendering flopping panfish or bass into crisp, golden brown fillets.

While all states require occupants of watercraft to have floatation devices (life jackets) within handy reach, it is good policy to require kids to wear them at all times. There is a saying: "It is difficult to put on a life jacket when you are in the water; impossible on the bottom of a lake." If for some untoward reason a canoe with kids is swamped, the last thing adults need is to go floundering around to keep the kids afloat. Boy Scouts and Girl Scouts, in their canoe training, require youngsters to don swim suits and life jackets and to deliberately roll canoes over so they can get the feel of the mishap without any sense of panic. Not only do they gain an understanding of how a canoe swamps, but also learn procedure for getting the craft upright and floatable, getting the paddlers back aboard or swim to shore with it.

Very often, when a canoe does dump, rods, reels, tackle boxes and everything else that is loose and sinkable, goes to the bottom. If the site is in shallow water, a few dives can usually locate the missing items. Deep water is something else, but not totally impossible. We have retrieved a number of lost rods by dragging very slowly over the area using another rod with a metal lure, like a Daredevle. The single treble hook makes a good grapple bumped over the bottom at the accident site and the lure will often snag onto the rod or line and the tackle is rescued.

All of this becomes the stuff of family legends: "Remember the time brother Joey dropped his fish rod in the lake and Grandpa got it back by dragging a metal lure over the bottom?"

When moving from one spot to another or when heading out on an expedition, three paddlers can move a canoe measurably faster than two. My preference is to have the third paddler seated directly behind the bow paddler so they can paddle opposite sides in unison without getting tangled up. The stern man paddles on whichever side seems to need the most thrust. We paddle at twenty strokes, then "hutt" to the opposite side. With three, like two, everyone needs to switch sides in unison.

Chapter Seven
BIG GAME GUNNERY BY CANOE

The Ojibwe did it with spears or bows and arrows. But as soon as they could swap beaver skins to the Voyageurs for muskets, they quickly opted for firearms. The woodland Indians were hunters. If they weren't stalking caribou, deer, moose, bear, or waterfowl, they were often hunting each other. Ojibwe with rifles made life so chancy for the Dakota that they moved out of the lake territory, across the Mississippi River and onto the plains. Here, these canoe paddlers became horse Indians, some of the best cavalry the world has ever seen.

The Ojibwe and other Great Lakes tribes were left to hunt in relative peace. Much of the fresh meat used by the early Voyageurs was harvested by canoe Indians with guns. Caucasian fur traders from Montreal certainly took a share of wild game along the trade routes, but it was much simpler and less time consuming to purchase it from the Indians. Eventually, the fur trade era ended. Settlers arrived who existed to a considerable extent on what they could shoot. In the 1800s the modern era of canoe hunting arrived. Outdoorsmen evolved their own methods of taking wildlife, methods still valid to a considerable extent.

26

In most states, it is not legal to shoot game from a motor-driven craft. It is legal to use a canoe and motor to get to a hunting area, but hunting is not permitted with a motor canoe although some states allow the motor to remain attached to the canoe but not running.

Thus canoe hunting is conducted in a traditional paddle-only mode. Indeed, the hunter moving quietly with a paddle is much more likely to ambush game than one roaring along in an outboard-powered craft. Certainly most of the best hunting is along shallow streams, through marshes and in shallow bays where a motor would be simply a hindrance if not impossible to use.

Canoe hunting can be either a solo or a two-person operation. When traveling solo, some hunters place a few large rocks in the bow to balance the craft and make handling easier. My preference is to sit in the bow seat facing backward, which puts my feet under the center thwart and my point of balance just behind the center. It takes a little harder 'push" on the J-stroke and more attention to detail, but it is easier to counter wind and waves from the center position. In a tough wind, it is possible to drop down on the knees just behind the center thwart and handle the craft from there.

Stalking solo, the rifle can be kept within easy reach with the stock resting on the canoe bottom, the barrel leaning against the center thwart to one side. As a right-handed shooter, I keep my weapon against the left gunwale, the stock by my left leg. It takes only a moment to scoop up the rifle with my left hand, flip off the safety, swing it against my shoulder and cut loose. It is often easier when kneeling, a position many take when completing a stalk.

When hunting with a companion, the shooter rests easily in the bow, gun ready, the canoe propelled mainly by the stern paddler who attends to nothing else. It is not only unsafe to have the stern paddler armed and ready to shoot, it is also unhandy. It takes experience and two steady hands to control the canoe and put the bow man in the best position to shoot. This applies equally where the hunters are easing along a winding timbered stream, seeking moose, or pushing softly through stands of wild rice or rushes trying to ambush a shoreline deer.

27

As noted before, the bow hunter stations himself sideways on a flat or cane-woven seat, one leg curled underneath, one shoved straight forward. The stern paddler not only directs the canoe to the best angle for a shot, but also remains ready to steady the craft with a paddle brace should the need arise. Both hunters concentrate on the target, marking accurately where the animal drops or where last seen near an identifiable tree, bush or rock. There is nothing more frustrating than to make a good shot and then flounder around for a half hour trying to find where the target fell or where it was standing when hit. Wounded moose often go crashing headlong through the understory, sometimes parallel to shore where a few strokes on the paddle may put the hunter in position for a second, killing shot. A deer hit along the shoreline will often bolt straight for the interior and a few strokes on the paddle, right or left, may allow a second view of the fleeing target with the shooter in position for a second shot.

With a large animal like a moose, many hunters use the rule: "If it aint near the shore, don't shoot." The idea is that moose provide a real chore when dressing one out, quartering it and moving it to the canoe for transport. If it is right on the water's edge, it is much easier to concentrate all of that effort. Also, many moose hunters carry along a block and tackle or come-along with which to winch the moose up on the bank if it drops in the water. There is nothing more difficult than attempting to quarter a moose which is lying belly-deep in a sea of loon doo-doo.

Most of us, if we have our druthers, will opt for a stormy day when hunting. In a tough wind, snow or rain, it is usually much easier to approach close to moose or deer on the shore. Both animals tend to hesitate when staring into a storm, trying to ascertain just what is approaching. That moment's hesitation is usually all it takes. Fog is also a good weather cover for a stalk.

Al Ito, Win Hultstrand, my wife and I were after moose on the Kawishiwi River one fall, in a chill, damp daybreak encased with heavy fog. Al and Win were in one canoe, my wife and I in the other. We eased silently along opposite shores of the river, listening for the sound of water being stirred, the plop of a hoof and watching for telltale ripples which might indicate movement along shore. Win was paddling stern in their canoe, Al in the bow, rifle ready.

Prior to the hunt, Win, my wife and I determined that, if possible, we would try to get Al in position for a shot because up to that point he had never shot any sort of big game. As the bow of their canoe eased through the mist, Win detected tiny waves on the glassy surface, an indication that something was moving in the shallows. Next he heard a faint splash and a crunch, signal that an animal had stepped out of the river and was up on shore. In the mist, he spotted the faint outline of the moose, standing on a low ledge six feet above the river surface, watching the approach of the canoe.

Win reached forward slowly with his paddle and touched Al, motioning toward the ledge. Al peered straight into the mist, but at the waterline, not toward the ledge above where the moose stood motionless. Concerned that the animal would bolt, Win poked Al again, aimed his paddle at the moose and whispered tersely: "For heaven's sake, Al, shoot!"

And that sound, the moose shuffled toward the dense forest at which point Al spotted it, swung up his rifle and cracked off a shot.

29

The huge animal stumbled and went crashing into the understory. "You nailed him!" Win grunted, shoving the canoe up on the closest piece of beach. Both men jumped out to search.

Hearing some branches break down the shore to his right, Win cut through a point of timber and found the moose sprawled dead on the shoreline. But he couldn't see Al anywhere.

"Al!" he called. "Al, where the heck are you?'

At this point, we must return to the moose hunt briefing provided by the Minnesota Department of Natural Resources for all hunters prior to the season. Every group of hunters getting a Minnesota moose permit is required to attend an orientation session concerning the hunting laws and also for a crash course with photos showing where to shoot a moose for best effect and how to dress out the kill.

At the Ely briefing, the DNR spokesman explained how a sure killing shot can be delivered just back of the shoulder where it will pierce the heart or lungs. "If hit in the lungs, the animal may go 150 paces or so and then drop," he noted.

Thus, after Al fired, he jumped out on the shore and began stepping off 150 paces in the fog-shrouded woods. Meanwhile, Win had located the dead moose and yelled: "Where the heck are you?"

"I'm stepping off 150 paces," Al replied from back in the forest.

"Never mind that," Win yelled back. "Come over here ... your moose is down dead."

Al crashed through the brush and arrived on the scene. "I don't think that's my moose," he observed.

It took Win a few minutes to convince Al that it was indeed his moose and the 150 pace thing was merely an example used by the game manager to indicate what might happen, not what did happen in this instance.

"It has to be your moose," Win confided. "There are no other hunters around and no other shots. Besides, it's the one I saw standing on the ledge as we came up."

In any event, it was a plump young critter of perhaps 700 pounds that provided some tasty moose steaks in the coming winter.

Most canoe hunters carry a good pair of field glasses to scan the shoreline. In any case, a canoe moving with as little disturbance as possible, can be brought within rifle range relatively easy. However, if the target appears nervous, it may be best to beach the craft out of view and complete the stalk on foot. The only trouble with this is that the snap of a branch or crunch of brush underfoot may well spook the animal before a shot can be accomplished. It's a judgment call.

In Northern Minnesota and Western Ontario where we hunt, we sometimes tow a canoe for several miles behind a motorboat to reach a remote area. When we arrive at the hunting site, we beach the motorboat and take to the paddle craft. This allows us to hunt some distance into the wild country, away from other hunters. It also provides a motorized means of transporting our game home if we are lucky.

In deer hunting, we sometimes stalk with the canoe, but usually use it as a means to set up our hunt. Often, one hunter will be dropped off along the river bank or lake shore and the other paddles the canoe a half mile or so upwind. This hunter beaches the canoe and moves inland, locating on a ridge or crossing along a well-used trail. The first hunter then works his way slowly upwind, perhaps pushing a buck into the hunter ahead or catching one attempting to circle back. Our best case scenario is when we have an early snow, allowing us to track our deer, teaming up on foot and by canoe to bag our venison.

The nice thing about the canoe is that it makes the job easy to haul the deer to the boat and home. On the other hand, extreme care must be taken in wintry conditions. A slip on a snowy rock and a dunking in ice water can be quite uncomfortable. Care must be taken with 180 pounds of buck deer loading down a canoe in wind and waves. A good survival kit with matches in a waterproof case is essential. Care must also be taken to insure that the outboard on the boat is in top running condition for winter weather, the gas is clean and ice-free. Also, word should be left with a responsible third party as to where the hunt is being conducted and the expected time of return noted so help can be organized in case of motor trouble and the hunters do not get back. Of course, with a canoe, hunters can always paddle back in an emergency. But it is well to eliminate every possible outside chance for something to go wrong.

Chapter Eight

SMALL GAME

A raw northwest wind moaned through the fir tops, whipped skeins of snow across the black surface of Gun Lake and rattled the taut nylon tarp that sheltered our small cook stove. The tarp, roped between several accommodating balsam. An aspen ridge pole was rigged like a front porch to our tent. When weather roared in, we had a dry exit and entry to the tent and a dry adjacent cooking area.

The propane stove hissed and sputtered, an aluminum coffee pot resting on one burner, a frying pan bubbling with bacon on the other. Doc Spangler squinted into the windswept darkness, hands cradling a steaming coffee cup, head cocked to one side.

"Mallards movin' out there," he commented.

My wife and I stepped to the edge of the tarp. Distinct from the waves slapping the shoreline, we detected the rhythmic beat of feathered pinions in the predawn gloom coupled with the faint "cutta-cutta-cut" gabble of greenheads moving to the wild rice beds. Doc grinned, finished his coffee and administered a dozen or so pumps to the hissing Coleman lantern. "The trouble with a trip like this, "said Doc, surveying the cozy scene, "Is that it has to end sometime."

Our camp was a few miles from the Minnesota-Ontario border

33

in an area frequented by fleets of canoe campers in the summer; but in October, we hadn't seen another soul all week. This is no local phenomenon. Once September's golden days are gone, the canoe trails of the north are deserted except for the occasional hunter or trapper. Some weather hazards are to be expected, of course, but there are many plusses.

First is a complete absence of the little winged vampires that fly and bite, eliminating the need for protecting creams, sprays or nets. Airborne microspores no longer torment the respiratory tracts of the allergic. Deep green spruce and pine set a contrasting background for bright golden birch and aspen, accented here and there with fiery splashes of scarlet maple. At dawn, wraiths of blue mist, like ghosts of ancient Ojibwe warriors, dance along the dim shorelines. On clear nights, as frost is brushed in broad white strokes on rocks and logs, stars crowd down for a closer look at the vast, dark forest. It is a time when the outdoors is battening down for winter, when nature's migrants are on the move toward warmer climes, when resident species don thickened coats for the approaching freeze-up. It is also a time for the human animal to renew mind and soul. Which was why we happened to be on Gun Lake.

Doc and I had grown up on the same street, gone to the same schools, hunted the same marshes and uplands, fished and canoed the same rivers until our paths had parted. He went on to Northwestern University Dental School, served with the medics in the Korean War, came home and subsequently opened a dental practice. In the meantime, I served a hitch with the Marines in WW II, got married, spawned a couple of daughters and put in 16 years covering the outdoor scene for three different newspapers before migrating to northern Minnesota to open a canoe outfitting and guiding service. One day a letter arrived from Doc saying he had grown old and tired as a tooth carpenter and felt perhaps he was due a respite from the dental problems of the world, perhaps a brief time to heft a spinning rod, sight down the barrel of a shotgun and maybe hark to the haunting cry of a timberwolf pack on a moonlight hunt..

On the trail, it took about three days for the fluorescent-light, city look to vanish from Doc's eyes, three days of busting ruffed grouse out of hazel nut thickets, whipping jutjawed smallmouth bass on the deep side of rock reefs and jumping-shooting mallards out of rice-choked mud bottom bays. In three days he shed 30 years.

Our camp was pitched in a small, sandy clearing, sheltered on three sides by protecting trees and open toward the south to absorb any available sunlight. Our steep-roofed "A" tent was designed to shed both rain and snow. Zipped shut at night, it was warm as a cocoon. Our 14x16 nylon kitchen tarp was pitched taut over a smooth aspen ridgepole from which hung the gas lantern. A large flat rock supported our cook stove and two peeled pine logs provided seating on either side of the stove. A line strung beneath the tarp accommodated wet jackets and pants for drying. The gas lantern was also used sparingly inside the tent at night to help eliminate the chill while we crawled into our sleeping bags

Along with foam pads and sleeping bags, the tent contained items of necessity such as flashlights, toilet paper, candles, extra sox and underwear. A small whisk broom was used to sweep out snow, leaves and twigs. We also kept our food pack in the tent since bears had long gone into hibernation.

On the ground at the edge of the tarp we cleared away a circle of leaves and pine needles and erected a rock fireplace where we could safely kindle a wood fire, a blaze that doubled as a clothes drier and body warmer on chill nights. With the camp snugged down, we turned our attention to the pursuit of fish and game.

Our watercraft was an 18-foot lightweight Grumman, painted flat tan, a slow, wide-beamed hull with ample capacity for three and adequate stability with little chance of swamping, an important consideration in the fall when the lakes are turning ice cold. Some north country shooters, wear oversize hunting jackets which can camouflage brightly-colored life jackets. We had no concern with this since our old, soiled life vests had no bright color left to spook even the most wary migrants. We wore them over our hunting jackets.

Most canoe hunters are aware of chilly water, but not as many

35

consider the cold weather hazard of dehydration and fatigue. We nibbled periodically on gorp and dried fruit, drank frequent cups of water and used a hot pot of soup to fortify our noon lunch. On one-day, non-wilderness hunts, we sometimes carry hot soup in a thermos. Often, two thermoses, one with coffee.

Decoys consisted of a dozen inflatable rubber mallards and another dozen bluebills, all of which could be rolled up and stowed in a single Duluth pack with enough room left over for lunch. The mallard decoys, spaced in an opening among wild rice patches, handled the puddle ducks. The bluebill decoys, clustered off rocky points, were sufficient to toll scaup, ringbills, goldeneye or bufflehead. Northern Minnesota wilderness waterfowl, while not nearly as numerous as those in the Dakotas, are also not as sophisticated as the same birds encountered further south after becoming wary of duck boats, blinds and decoys; but they do not wing in with surrender flags unfurled, either. Upon locating a busy duck crossing, we made a temporary blind of balsam brush with an old minnow seine, floats and lead sinkers removed, draped over the branches to afford concealment.

Wilderness waterfowl shooting has a unique problem in that there are few if any other hunters around to keep the birds moving. Thus we were required to spend considerable time scouting for flocks in the rice or, searching for bluebills feeding on crustaceans and shellfish in shallow bays. When decoy action simply did not occur, we moved out quietly and engaged in jump shooting, first tossing a coin to determine who would hold down the shooter's seat in the bow. A few times, when we spotted small flocks of divers along exposed shores where a stalk was impossible, we left one person on a prominent point of land, then two of us cruised downwind along the far shore rousting out the ducks which invariably made a swing upwind and crossed the point where the shooter was afforded a passing shot.

A couple of mornings, we paddled up small meandering streams like Moosecamp Creek, rimmed with tall reeds which afforded cover for our approach. In all, we bagged enough ducks for two dinners plus Doc's limit to take home. In the chill weather, there was no concern that any of our dressed fowl would spoil. They kept well.

One-Handed Stalk

When hunting alone, I sometimes pack along a small, one-handed blade, like a large ping pong paddle. Rafts of diving ducks can be stalked at an angle from upwind, the shooter kneeling, body low, eyes just even with the gunwale. Scaup and other divers will often sit nervously as the canoe slowly approaches, paddled by one arm on the side away from the birds' vision. Drifting in with the tailwind, the canoe often glides within range before the nervous birds take to the air. Since divers invariably jump upwind, this means they are coming at the shooter, at least for the first few yards, narrowing the range even more.

When the ducks are airborne, the paddle is dropped and the shotgun brought up smartly. A thong connects the paddle handle to the center thwart so it won't drift away.

We dress our birds almost immediately after shooting them, while they are still warm, to quickly chill them down. Regulations in regard to portaging ducks vary among the different states, usually requiring heads and wings to be left intact for identification. On a short trip, we may also pluck the birds but on longer trips we leave the feathers intact to keep the birds from drying out.

In November, it is quite common for ice to form on the canoe and on the paddles. A pair of rubber gloves stuck in the duffle can be a finger-saver when handling decoys or downed birds. We always pull the canoe up and turn it over at night so any water inside will drain out, not form ice and if a blizzard arrives, snow won't pile up inside the hull. Paddles placed in the shelter of the tarp will stay ice-free.

Ice along shore can create treacherous footing on rocks and logs. We load up with the stern paddler getting in the canoe, facing back, both hands free. Gear and guns are handed to him and carefully stowed before the bow shooter climbs in. When the shore is slippery, we sometimes secure the canoe to a shoreline tree or log with a line to the center thwart. A line so tied can save a lot of grief.

One late October afternoon, in a driving snowstorm, my wife and I beached our canoe at the foot of a campsite where we intended to spend the night. It had been snowing all day and we were chilled, thus in a hurry to empty the canoe, pitch the tent and get a fire kindled. My wife picked up one packsack and headed for the campsite while I grabbed another and trudged up the slippery bank. With both of us out and the packs removed, the lightened craft slipped backward on the icy shore and started downwind alone. There was a clutch at my gut when I recognized the situation, but the options were few.

Peeling off my clothes and boots, I hit the ice water, striking out for the drifting canoe even though most of my breath was stuck just under my Adam's apple. When I reached the errant craft, I looped one arm over the gunwale and swam back to shore, emerging at the campsite thoroughly numbed with no feeling from my navel down and shaking. With the canoe secured, I stumbled barefooted to the campsite where my wife had thoughtfully kindled a roaring blaze, which was fortunate because I was drifting toward hypothermia. Just that small mistake, like not securing the canoe properly, could have resulted in a serious problem. Anyone who allows his canoe to drift off should be diagnosed as terminally stupid.

North country grouse present canoemen with some excellent fall sport. Sometimes we hunt the summer campsites, paddling from one to the next, hoping to surprise a brace or so of these fine gamebirds which may be feeding on frost-ripened clover clumps in the clearings. Portage trails between lakes are also choice places to find ruffed rockets. Canoe country grouse seldom see hunters and are not nearly as spooky as their farmland cousins.

With both upland game and waterfowl, the canoe provides hunters with access to remote areas where game may be more abundant and hunting pressure minimal. In the Northern Minnesota wilderness areas where we hunt, quite often we go an entire day without hearing shots other than our own. Quite often we have embarked on hunts of a week or ten days, carrying only enough groceries to fill out meals built around roast duck or grouse. Having our fishing gear along, we alternate wildfowl with walleye, bass or northern pike fillets as fortune determines.

Chapter Nine

HOW CANOES TIP PEOPLE OVER

Although one may carefully examine countless canoes, it is difficult to locate one with a single muscle, tendon, blood vessel or indication of a nervous system. But canoes must somewhere have these physical attributes because they perversely "tip over" when people climb in, like broncos buck rodeo riders off.

During the years my wife and I outfitted and guided wilderness canoe trips, we had a variety of soggy folk ruefully relate how, in a fit of perversity, the canoe deposited passengers, fishing tackle and duffle into the water.

Oddly enough, no one has ever witnessed a canoe tipping over when empty. Apparently they sit docilely on the surface plotting treachery like a mean bronco waits quietly in the chute before the rider climbs onto the saddle. Then lookout! Similarly, when packsacks, fishing tackle and passengers or all three are added to canoes, they apparently commit acts of deviltry.

Let me confess, my wife and I have never experienced that phenomenon. Every time we were involved with a canoe mishap it was the result of what fliers call "P.E.," the abbreviation for "Pilot Error." The few times our canoe swamped were the result of some human miscalculation. In any event, all such occurrences prove one trait all canoes have in common: they leak. That is, they all leak over the top. Thus, whatever measures the canoeist can take to prevent such leakage is guaranteed to make the trip more pleasant.

The first possibility for trouble occurs when the paddlers, canoe and water all initially meet, usually when loading up. Where possible, it is wise to have the canoe resting in the water broadside to the beach, rock shelf or log landing. For safety, one canoeist steadies the craft by the gunwale while his companion carefully loads the packsacks between the thwarts, balancing the load so the canoe will ride level. If the canoe cannot be brought to shore broadside for loading and must be loaded while it is angling away, it can be situated so the stern is next to shore, the bow out in the water. While the stern paddler grips the gunwale to hold the craft steady, the bowman climbs inside, slides forward and positions himself just ahead of the center thwart where he drops to his knees to lower the center of gravity.

From this position, he can accept packsacks from his companion and stow them ahead and behind the center thwart. He can then accept paddles, tackle, guns or other loose items, and pack them aboard securely, turn around and sit down in the bow seat. The stern paddler then eases the craft out from shore, making the final push with one knee on the stern deck, then slides into the stern seat and prepares to get underway.

When the shoreline is so shallow that the loaded canoe will be aground, we simply wade out in our boots and load it while it is sitting empty in the water. Then, one at a time, the bowman climbs aboard, hesitating while the water runs out of his boots, then the stern paddler slides in and they push off. Some canoeists like to launch with a great push and a flying leap over the stern piece, a rather spectacular feat if the craft doesn't slam into a hidden rock or log pitching the acrobat into the water. Over the long haul, we find it drier and easier just to step in the canoe and sit down without any extra gymnastics.

There is one rule about getting in and out of a canoe which is not subject to amendment: When stepping in, the savvy canoeist leans over, grips the gunwales and places his first step directly on the centerline. Every time. When getting out, he leans over, grips the gunwales and with one foot on the centerline, places the other foot ashore. If the footing is firm, he may then safely transfer his weight to the shore foot If not firm, he will maintain his weight firmly on the back foot, will not lose his balance nor upset the canoe. No one but a rank amateur will stand up and stumble in or out of a canoe, particularly with his hands full of gear. Fishing tackle, guns, gear, whatever, are all left in the canoe until the bow man is out on solid ground. Then it is lifted or handed out, item by item.

When pulling into shore for the bow canoeist to get out, the stern paddler can hold the canoe steady with a paddle brace or with the blade anchored on the bottom. The canoe is always eased into shore. Ramming the bow into the bank can create a problem if a submerged rock or log is struck. Also, hitting the shore hard creates wear and tear on the bow piece and the hull. In addition, many a canoe is rolled over when the bow is run up on a steep shore where the bowman leaps out and pulls it up farther causing the craft to teeter precariously between the stern and that narrow portion of the hull still in the water.

In a moving canoe, the anglers or shooters always keep their rear ends centered on the seats. A person can lean outward, forward or back, move his arms or legs, but the tail end is always centered. Canoes with bucket seats anchor the paddler in place. Flat seats require a conscious effort to stay centered.

Guides dread a day on the water with a "butt shifter," a person who continually moves his center of gravity from one side to the other. In 1967, three days after ice-out, the teenage son of a neighbor and I were on Quetico Park's McAree Lake, fishing lake trout in the currents below Rebecca Falls. The fishing was good but the young man turned out to be not only a butt shifter but also a standupper, an unsettling turn of events with snow still on the ground and the water at about 40 degrees. Hooking his first seven-pound trout, he slid from gunwale to gunwale, then stood up, cranking furiously on his reel, while I cursed and paddle-braced first right, then left, yelling at him to sit down. He dropped back in place and I netted his fish. A moment later, he hooked another and went into a repeat performance. As I brought this fish to net I leaned forward and hissed: "You stand up one more time or even wiggle your tail end off the center of that seat, sonny, and I am going to take this paddle and tear your head clear off!" We had a reasonably safe and quiet day thereafter.

As noted, the canoe load is usually trimmed level, both from side-to-side and from bow-to-stern. However, the difference in weight between bow and stern paddlers must be considered and loads shifted accordingly. My wife weighs just about 100 pounds and I am 170, thus we tend to load a little heavier toward the bow. When rough water lies ahead, we drop to our knees to lower the center of gravity. In whitewater situations, it may pay to have the bow paddler kneel behind the bow seat to give the bow more buoyancy. If this is done, it must be anticipated so the packs can be shifted accordingly. However, in most instances, when we are trav-

43

eling with a load, we portage around almost all the whitewater rather than risk getting our gear wet.

One other thing: By law, we are required to have Coast Guard approved personal floatation devices, called PFDs, on board. These are what we used to call "life jackets," and will float a person but may not hold him totally upright with his head out of the water. Persons who cannot swim should wear a PFD at all times. In any case, when crossing rough water or running rapids, even good swimmers should have their PFD buckled on. If a canoe swamps, it is important to immediately check everyone to see that they are conscious, uninjured and swimming, not floating facedown.

When shopping for a PFD, try it on in the store to make sure it fits well and that all the zippers, ties, hooks and other closures are working. It may be a good idea to pick a paddle off the shelf and sit down in a chair to see how the jacket fits when swinging the paddle. Also, check the vest again while kneeling. A good PFD may cost as much as a medium priced paddle, but it is cheap life insurance and should last for ten years or more.

Some paddlers are expert swimmers and have no fear that they will be in trouble if the canoe fills with water. Sometimes canoeists tie their life jackets under the seats to keep them out of the way. This is a sensible move if the canoe is worth more than the people in it. Anyone who has been involved in a swamping will verify the following facts about life jackets: they are very difficult to buckle on when the canoeist is floating in the water and nearly impossible to put on when the canoeist is on the bottom of the lake.

Other than when pulled up against the shore for loading or unloading, canoes usually swamp in whitewater, which will be taken up later, or in a wind, which will be taken up right here. In any group discussion of wind and waves, somebody usually says: "I'd rather be in a canoe in rough water than in a boat." A couple of things are wrong with this observation: the first being that a canoe is a boat; the second is that a canoe is not built for use in high seas unless it happens to be a 34-foot Canot du Nord that the Montrealers used, or something similar. The best designed 16, 17 or 18-foot paddle craft is no match in rough water against a well-designed dory of the same length. An experienced canoeist does not get into waves that are dangerous. The trick is knowing which are and which aren't. This is often learned by trial and error ... or trial and luck.

A canoe without gear, loaded only with a pair of kneeling paddlers, can take two-foot, three-foot and even bigger waves if the paddlers are good. A fully-loaded canoe will ride lower in the water and handle more sluggishly. One way to learn about canoes in waves is to put on swimming suits and go out in the empty craft on a warm, windy day. One may practice paddling head-on into the waves, quartering, moving crosswind and downwind. This is an excellent way to pick up some rough water seamanship.

Heading straight into the waves will work in a chop, but in a heavy sea the bow will rise up over a crest and then drop with a smash. Quite often this results in water coming in over the gunwales at the bow seat. Usually, quartering into the waves at an angle, riding up and across the face of each wave and riding down the back is more stable and drier. Paddling is accelerated when the canoe is in the trough and when it hits the crest, a bow brace is applied at the peak, the stern paddler still churning. As the canoe goes over the top and down the back incline, the bow paddler drives his blade while the stern paddler braces.

Observation will show that every fourth or fifth wave is the biggest, the one that is likely to "getcha." Thus the teamwork of paddling and bracing probably needs be applied mostly on those big combers.

Very often trouble occurs when running with the wind, especially coming off a lee shore where the canoeists are reading the backs of big waves. From a distance, these waves may not look particularly large, but there may be indications of rough water if the tree tops are bending and waves can be observed cracking against the shore some distance downwind. The problem with heading out in a back wind is that once committed, there is usually no turning back. Attempting to turn in a high backwind puts the paddlers in danger of broaching and swamping. A downwind ride can be exhilarating but risky. Before getting into "the stuff" some canoeists load their craft a trifle bow heavy to make the stern ride higher. In all such cases, we drop forward on our knees and lower the center of gravity.

Running with the waves, the canoe will pick up speed as it climbs the crest. Then it slows down abruptly as it goes over the crest and rides down the reverse face before picking up the next wave. It is possible to get up enough speed to pick up a good comber and "surf" for some distance, but once the forward speed is cut, the danger comes from the following wave breaking over the stern. It is good procedure to try this out with swim suits, long before an extended cruise on big water.

Rather than get into a rough surf, one may simply take a nap and wait for the wind to blow itself out. We have spent many an hour with the canoe pulled up on shore, coffee cup in hand, watching the wind blow and waves crash rather than getting out into the maelstrom.

If the course is upwind and decision is made to move on, a study of the map and the terrain may allow a course to be charted taking advantage of islands and points. Wind acts much like running water in that it swirls behind obstructions creating eddies. A headwind coming around a point of land may have a strong reverse air current along the lee side which the canoeists may pick up and ride upwind. Waves breaking across a point will often be sharper and meaner than out farther, thus it is usually well to attack at a long, quartering angle, the bowman paddling on the upwind side, stern man on the lee side so the bow paddler can draw, if necessary to keep heading into the wind.

In any rough sea, some slop will come in. If gear is sealed against water, it will stay dry. Prior to the advent of plastic pack liners, old timers laid a few two-inch saplings on the canoe bottom which created a "bilge" that allowed the packs to ride high and dry. A little slop is no problem, but if it builds up, particularly in a flat bottom canoe it can shift and cause capsizing. Some paddlers carry a boat sponge jammed up under a pack strap. Dry, they weigh nothing; but are excellent for sopping up excess water. In a big sea, we break out a cook pail for a bailer, tying it to the canoe with a

46

three-foot leash so it won't vanish if dropped accidentally over the side. Some canoeists use an empty gallon bleach jug with the bottom cut out for a bailing bucket.

Lashing Packs In The Canoe

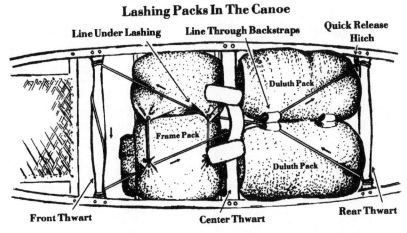

In any confrontation with big water, it is essential that packs, tackle or guns be lashed securely in the canoe. When a canoe swamps, it fills to the gunwales and becomes a sodden, unwieldy hulk. Packs, rod cases or gun cases not lashed in may go riding off downwind to heaven knows where- or they may fill with water and sink Some old-timers fastened in packs by unbuckling shoulder straps and looping them over the thwarts, then buckling them back to the pack. We prefer a section of nylon rope, crisscrossed over the packs and through the straps, culminating with a quick release hitch on the thwart. If a swamped canoe gets blown onto a rocky, windswept shore, it may be necessary to get the packs out quick and lighten the hull before the waves smash it to pulp.

In the spring and fall, when the water temperature may be well below 50 degrees, swamping is not a funny business. Survival time in water that cold may be anywhere from 5 to 15 minutes. It may be prudent to travel within easy reach of the shore even though it may add an extra mile to the trip. A spill in this situation means getting to shore promptly. Every canoeist should carry matches in a waterproof case so a fire can be started immediately and the paddlers warmed up. A cold, wet situation can cause hypothermia with shaking, stupor, convulsions and death.

Sometimes a person will run across a book that advises: "When waves get too big, simply lie down on the bottom of the canoe and its natural buoyancy will ride the waves out."

Sure it will. Just how two paddlers with a canoe full of duffle are supposed to find a place to lie down is never explained. Furthermore, there is no reason to think a drifting canoe will remain afloat just because some terrified paddlers are stretched out on the bottom.

Frankly, we often enjoy the exhilaration of a good, howling gale, the canoe pitching and bucking with spray blowing off the tops of the whitecaps; but we know what we can handle and what we can't. Many times we have waited out a storm and, if necessary, paddled all night when the wind went down.

Chapter Ten
SUDS

Old timers have a saying: "Nobody ever drowned on a portage."

It might also be added that few paddlers ever lost their canoe, tent, sleeping bags, cook kit, food, guns or fishing tackle while taking a detour on foot around a set of rapids. But, like the mountain climber who goes for the peak "because it's there" most cruising canoeists, sooner or later, will point the nose of their craft into a stretch of whitewater. The choice is even easier for canoeists: Rapids are all down hill.

While steelhead fishing in British Columbia with resident guide-angler-mountaineer Tim Timmins some years ago, we paused for a breather on the rim of a stream that elbowed, kicked and bulled its way down to the Pacific in a spectacular display of thunderous suds. "I wonder," I questioned aloud, "if a couple of guys could run that stretch in a canoe?"

"Sure," Tin answered thoughtfully. "They could once."

And that is the literal truth about any set of rapids. They can be run once. But there is no guaranteeing the condition of the canoe, outfit or personnel at the exit. Shooting a stretch of current and froth can be an adrenaline-charging kick for experienced paddlers who know their canoe, their own ability and can judge at a glance if there is a navigable avenue through. But the chances are, they didn't learn their skills on a wilderness camping trip by a risking a canoe load of gear. They learned in a empty canoe, with safety devices, and most probably with someone experienced in whitewater.

It is nowhere required that cruising campers, anglers or hunters be competitive whitewater experts. Few are. But they should have a working knowledge of how their craft reacts in a current, what paddle strokes may be required to get through turbulent water and possess an ability to "read" moving water - to accurately judge whether a given stretch can be safely navigated. Time to go for practice.

The ideal craft for whitewater is a smooth-bottomed, keel-less hull, ample of beam, high in buoyancy and rockered fore and aft. Slick, tough plastic and fiberglass take the bangs well and slide over rocks easier than metal which tends to grab and stick. Buoyancy is determined by length, width, flare, tumblehome and good floatation. A rockered and keel-less bottom allows the craft to be turned abruptly, even spun on its axis and slipped from side to side.

Don't own a whitewater canoe? We don't, either. So we will get in the river with what we own because that is what we will be cruising in.

Naturally both paddlers will be wearing PFDs. And if we can, we borrow or beg tough plastic helmets because we don't want our skulls cracked on underwater rocks. If it is spring or fall with cold water a certain prospect, we will also borrow a couple of wet suits so we don't wind up hypothermic. And we will go with at least one more team of canoeists so somebody will be ashore or afloat to offer assistance if we really get in a bind.

OK? All set? Let's push off, paddle to the middle of the stream and head downcurrent. According to our map there is some kind of a drop ahead, but not a very steep one, so we are looking and listening for it. The first indication appears as a line across the water surface. As we look down the stream sides, we see trees, brush and rocks coming down to the shore. But straight ahead, at that line across the water, realize we are looking at the trees from a point part way up on the trunks. The shore, tree roots and rocks are below our vision. Moving closer, we see a few flicks of foam or waves on the lip of the drop and we hear water gurgling. So we pick a nice, flat place to land and get out for a look.

What we have ahead is merely a riffle that slides down through some gravel deposits, just a nice current to ride through. But, wait a minute. What is that sound around the bend: We walk a little further and see where the stream has now narrowed down and is pulsing through rows of boulders, a "rock garden" in river parlance. On the left we note where the main force of the current is moving through a sufficiently deep, unobstructed channel and below that is a long stretch of quiet water.

Fine. Now we know we can safely float down the drop, keep to the left and pick our way through the rock garden. We make a mental note that if we come through in low water, we could probably have to rope down instead of riding.

We paddle our craft to the main current, pick the "V" where the water enters the rapids, ride down the left channel, through the rock garden and sail clear - with just one loud thump as the hull bounces off a submerged boulder we didn't see. A fleeting glimpse shows some paint and some aluminum on the rock, so ours isn't the first canoe that ever made contact there.

Ahead, the river narrows and we see another line across the water with quite a few little whiffs of spray bounding in the sunlight and a more insistent roar. Again, we beach our craft, get out and take a look. Stretching nearly all the way across the stream is a level rock formation, a "ledge" which is something like a dam. Water is very shallow on top of the ledge. Where it drops in three feet below, there is a lot of turbulence with the current churning back against the ledge. If we try to go over the ledge, we stand a good chance of getting stuck, broaching and rolling over. If we clear the ledge, we may wind up in the backwash below where we could get rolled around for some time. We don't buy it

But on the near side of the ledge we spot a break in the rock, a "chute" where the main force of the water is booming through. It is a straight, fast slick halfway down, but in the middle there's a big boulder with water piling up in front, bouncing over its top and

51

churning to the bottom of the rapids in a series of foamy waves that merge in a row of "haystacks" - standing waves where the current ends its wild dash into quiet water.

OK, we're on our way. We drop to our knees to lower our center of gravity, line up for the chute and start down, having decided to take the right side of the big rock. But wait a minute! As we start, the current starts dragging us over in line with the rock. The bowman is paddling furiously to get right and he does; but the current now has a good shot at the stern and the canoe is descending at an angle. The bow clears the rock, but the horrified stern man, flailing wildly, barely has time to yell: "Look out!" when Bam! The craft hits, teeters a moment, then leans upstream. The river pours in over the upstream gunwale. In a flicker, canoe, gear and paddlers are awash.

We have done our homework, so we don't panic. We get out of the craft upstream so the swamped hull with a half ton of water won't come crashing down to pin us against the rocks below. And we flipped over on our backs, heels downstream, so anything we hit will be cushioned by our feet and not our heads. A good thing, too, because we go clear under in the foam momentarily, feel rocks ricocheting off the soles of our boots before we both wind up at the base of the haystacks. Our friends, who portaged around, are on the shore doubled up with mirth. Eventually they paddle out, retrieve us and our swamped craft. If nothing else, we've learned a few things.

Foundering canoes do not usually "roll over" in a current. What happens is that the force of the current passing under the hull pulls the upstream gunwale down and that's where the water pours in. Thus a keel canoe not only hangs up on rocks easier, but also gives the current more leverage. And we've found that we had better be lined up correctly as we move into the chute. If we're not, we may not have time to correct our error.

We have also found that a life vest provides buoyancy only in "solid" water. In foam, we sank to the bottom, vest and all, which may explain why people who go over dams or steep ledges sometimes don't come up even through they were wearing PFDs. Luck-

52

ily, we were mostly in solid water and largely floated. We wipe the water off our faces, dump out the canoe, carry it back up and run the same stretch again. Only this time, we line up a little better. As we start moving toward the chute, we see that the current has that side motion, drawing us to the left in line with that boulder again. Only now we back paddle, angling the stern slightly to the right so that the current pushes us to the right. We "ferry" sideways in the slick and ease 'er down, back-paddling to the right or left to shift the canoe sideways in the current and around the boulder. As the canoe skids sideways, it remains lined up with the current. We bounce through the haystacks, we come though high and dry, which is what we should have done the first time.

So we rode down a chute, safely negotiated a short drop. But we had better not get too adventurous before we attempt something more involved. Even a little drop can wreck a canoe.

Just a few miles from our home is a small piece of water called Splash Lake. At the outlet are some weathered timbers remaining from an ancient logging sluice, circa 1910 or so. A moderate out-flow of water winds 200 yards through rapids and rocks into Newfound Lake. Around these rapids is a well-used portage trail over which dozens of canoeists annually walk; but a few would rather ride. Thirty feet below the sluice outlet lies an underwater ledge. To avoid the ledge requires a quick angle across the current and perhaps some luck. Some make it. Some don't. Twice we've been there when somebody's luck went sour.

The first featured two young men in a brand new Old Town, less than two weeks old, according to the owner. Time was mid-May, high water and cold. The men were loading their gear and tackle into the canoe at the top of this chute. Without trying to appear too nosey, we suggested that maybe the portage was a little more secure. We were assured that they knew exactly what they were doing, that they would "shoot" across the current to miss the ledge, etc. We sat down and leaned against a couple of trees to watch.

With the bowman in place, the stern paddler pushed off with a mighty shove. Maybe not mighty enough. The canoe swept down

53

sideways, whacked the ledge, filled up, jammed between two rocks and broke amidships, the two men gasping and flailing in the ice water. Other than skinned knees and wet clothes, the men were all right. We helped them retrieve their wrecked canoe, packs and other gear, although they lost some rods and reels. And since we had a motorboat cached nearby, we hauled them and their now defunct Old Town to the nearest Forest Service public landing. Other than chattering teeth, they were pretty silent all the way.

At that same exact spot, one year later, Ely druggist Lee Schumacher and I were portaging across and saw two young men with a 17-foot Grumman canoe from Bernie Carlson's Quetico-Superior Outfitters preparing to make that same cross-current assault. Unable to dissuade them from their venture, we hurried with our camera to a point below and captured the event on film - the push-off, the impact with the ledge, water pouring into the craft and an ice water baptism by immersion. In this case, the canoe sustained only a few dents and the paddlers suffered no damage other than to their pride. At the foot of the rapids, Lee and I waded out, grabbed their swamped canoe, packsacks, and any other gear floating past. The only things missing were a couple of fishing rods and a couple of aluminum drinking cups that drifted off. Outside of being wet, they weren't in much trouble, so they emptied the water out of the canoe and paddled back to the outfitter's. This wasn't exactly the story they told Bernie, but that's how it really happened.

The years we were in the outfitting business, my wife and I credited three canoes to that little rapids, one a brand-new, 15-foot Grumman, totaled on its first trip. Anyone who doesn't understand running water will look at that stretch and swear it is a piece of cake. The ledge is just one little flaw in that observation, but it's an important flaw.

Canoeists who have never racked up in a chute cannot possibly grasp the terrific impact of a swamped canoe when it hits an underwater obstruction. A dry canoe, floating high, will usually bounce off a rock or log; but a swamped canoe, with perhaps three fourths of a ton of water inside (compute it out!) will break, collapse or

54

even wrap around a sunken rock like a strip of tinfoil or plastic. Hundred of artifacts - bow sections, ribs, canvas, strips of plastic or aluminum - decorate North America's major canoe routes from Texas to the Arctic, testimony to the power of currents against swamped hulls.

But back to business. Many canoeists, upon approaching an unknown rapids, will portage the packs and gear across, studying the river course before going back for the canoe. If the decision is made to run the strip, it can be done without the weight and bulk of the packs and with some knowledge of what's ahead.

Some years back, Ontario guide-outfitter Bud Dickson and I were on the Turtle River, south of Bending Lake, a stream with some pretty fair drops, perhaps two-thirds of them negotiable. One of these sticks out in my mind, not because it was particularly dif-

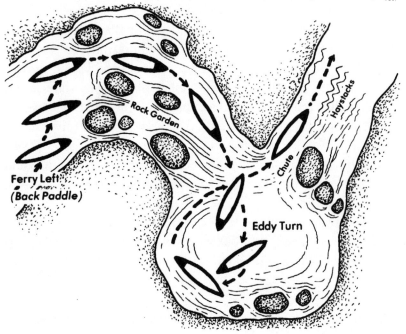

ficult, but because of the variety of water.

We carried our packs across, then walked the stream bank, eyeing the current. From the top, it eased off glassy and smooth, tilted into a rock garden that curved to the right, then poured into a small pool with a churning, foaming outlet that left the pool at a sharp angle. We figured we would ship some water in the rock garden and would need to make a pause at the pool, dump out the excess water, then ferry up and across the current to line up on the outlet chute to hit the left edge and miss most of the turbulence. That's how we played it. Negotiating the rock garden, we bounced off a few donnickers, shipped two inches of slop, hit the eddy in the bottom pool and pulled in. We beached, emptied out the water, pushed back into the current, ferried across to the left shore, lined up on the left of the big drop and ran through the foam, with standing waves towering higher than our heads on the right gunwale. In the calm below, we paddled to shore and picked up our packs. We had both agreed on strategy prior to the run. Had there been a disagreement, we would have carried the canoe around. Once in a rapids, there is no time for debate.

"Fine," says the guy from Indiana, Iowa or Illinois. "But where do we find that kind of water to practice in down here?"

But there are rapids in farm country streams, especially in spring's flood water. In March and April, rainfall fills drainage ditches and comes boiling out of field tiles turning those meandering cow-pasture streams into raging torrents. We grew up down there, running swollen rivers, dodging fence posts and fallen trees, ferrying to miss bridge abutments, cutting behind flooded hog feeders and hay bailers and plunging over old dams. Some of those rides were very exciting.

There are excellent whitewater books available through local book stores, illustrated books which are for beginners as well as experts. One may not intend to do any white water canoeing, but a knowledge of how canoes act in a current should be part of everyone's repertoire.

Again, if the canoe has gear aboard, it should be securely lashed in. Packs, fishing tackle and guns need to be secured to the canoe, guns especially. Over the years we have accidentally hooked into several fishing outfits that somebody lost in various rapids and one deer rifle with the wooden stock weathered away. Never knew who lost these items, but some paddlers had some very bad experiences.

56

One Man Lining Upstream

Chapter 11
LINING AND POLING

When negotiating a swift current, it is not always necessary to paddle or portage around. Canoeists for centuries have "lined" both up and down, although lining up is a lot less hazardous. This method of avoiding a portages is accomplished by lashing a single, quarter-inch nylon rope to two points on the canoe, preferably one end on the bow ring or loop and the other to the middle or stern thwart. In a moderate current, one man can handle the single line as long as the shore is not too rugged. Otherwise, two ropes are used with two men working the canoe forward in steps. The trick is to keep the bow angled slightly into the current with a both lines taut, moving slowly upstream. Pressure on the canoeist's arms will indicate if this is a feasible move. If the current is too swift, the angle may be changed slightly and the canoe brought to shore where it can be pulled out and portaged across.

Lining downstream is precarious since there is no real way to gauge the power of the current until the canoe is out in it. If the current is too strong to handle, one of two things may happen, both of them bad: 1. The canoeist is forced to let go of the rope and the craft goes wildcatting uncontrolled down the chute. 2. The canoeist tries to hang onto the rope and gets yanked off the shore to go wildcatting down the chute along with the canoe. Where they wind up and in what condition is anybody's guess. We always figured that if we couldn't ride a canoe down a rapids, we portage it and not try to sneak it through on a rope leash.

Canoeists who spend a lot of time on rivers, particularly in the east, do as much poling as paddling. This may be a much older means of moving a canoe since primitive men probably pushed log rafts and dugouts around with saplings long before anyone figured out how to carve a paddle. In any event, poling is experiencing somewhat of a comeback in those areas where shallow streams abound. In the 1930s, I spent my summers on Illinois' Fox River, fetching and carrying for a maiden aunt school teacher who had a cottage two miles downriver from the Village of Yorkville. My mode of transport was an 18-foot Old Town wood-and-canvas Guide Model which I poled upstream to Yorkville for groceries and downstream to the cottage and points beyond. By trial and error, sheer luck and some wet clothes, I learned how to stand back of the center thwart, one leg braced against the stern thwart, the other forward, the 12-foot iron-shod point of the pole trailing for a series of quick jabs or a long push. Going upstream, I usually planted the butt solidly on the bottom and then "climbed" the pole, hand-over-hand. When I came to the end of the pole, I quickly swung it forward, planted it and proceeded to climb it again. Coming downstream, I sat down, using either the pole or the paddle, since standing was too precarious in the event the canoe rammed a rock or a log.

Poling in the North Country is usually connected with harvesting wild rice because it is impossible to shove a canoe through thickets of rice with a paddle. The pole is shod with a "duckbilled" shoe which consists of two metal "bills" hinged at the center. When shoved underwater the duck bill opens up providing a solid base for shoving against the muck and submerged roots. The Indians

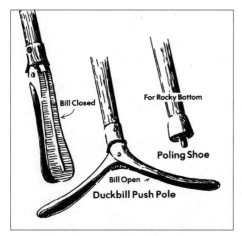

Bill Closed

For Rocky Bottom

Poling Shoe

Bill Open

Duckbill Push Pole

harvested rice by pushing the canoe through the stalks using a forked tree limb, but the duckbilled shoe is a heck of an improvement.. When the pole it is lifted, the duck bill folds in against itself and moves easily ahead for a the next thrust.

When gathering rice, everyone - Ojibwe or white men - use the same system: The pole man, standing erect by the stern seat, shoves the canoe ahead slowly into the stalks. On his knees, near the center thwart, his companion wields two ricing sticks about 30 inches long. With one arm, he reaches out and hooks a sheaf of stalks with one stick, bends them over the gunwale and knocks the grain loose and into the hull with the other stick. When wild rice is ripe, in late August or September a fleet of ricers in freshly-scrubbed canoes invade the vast stands of greenish-brown stalks, gathering up to 200 pounds of grain in each canoe for a half day's effort. A half day is about as long as anyone can wish to endure kneeling on the canoe bottom. When ricing is completed, the grain is bagged, the push pole stowed inside the canoe, the ricers pick up their paddles and head for home.

Where duck hunting is conducted over wild rice beds, hunters often use a duckbilled push pole to get their canoe through the heavy stands of stalks to retrieve downed ducks. There is no better fall feast than roast duck served up on a bed of wild rice dripping with orange gravy. Unless, maybe a little later on, it is a couple of venison tenderloins steaming on the same bed of wild rice.

Chapter Twelve
OTHER MEANS OF TRAVEL

Records indicate that a fisherman named C. B. Waterhouse invented the first outboard motor at Detroit, Michigan in 1905 and began to market motors in 1906. While Waterhouse made his outboard "kicker" to work on rowboats, it was not long before some canoe angler sawed two feet of canvas and planking off the stern of his craft, added a wood transom and started a new phase of canoeing.

There are drawbacks to motorized canoe use, one of them being added weight. Because square sterns need more bracing, they weigh more than paddle canoes. Even with a side bracket on a lightweight paddle canoe, outboard motors can add upwards of 24 pounds to the load and five gallons of gas weigh 40 pounds. It takes as much gas to get back from some place as it takes to get there.

Even with a side bracket on a lightweight paddle canoe, the weight difference of adding a motor and gas is considerable, but a lot of people use them. In many areas, particularly in the far north and up to the edge of the Arctic, motor canoes are the aquatic pickup trucks of trappers, fishermen, hunters and freight haulers. Over time, at least 25 canoe makers in North America turned out some 38 models of square stern and "T" backs and there is no count of how many paddle canoe models have been fitted with side brackets.

Matching the motor to the canoe is as important as matching the canoe to the job. In Canada's far north, Cree trappers and freighters have long used big Peterboro square backs with 10-horsepower motors and they portage these outfits all over. But then, we have seen these same individuals regularly pack 400 pounds of freight on their backs up the ramps at Hudson Bay Company loading docks. In a few instances, we have used a 10-horse on a 17-foot aluminum square back, but it is not the peak of stability.

Some of my more burly neighbors used to travel long distances on fishing weekends with big, 19-foot Grumman square sterns and 9.9 motors on the back. A few of the hardier anglers did not even take the motor off the transom when portaging. To balance the load, they lashed the six-gallon gas tank up under the bow seat.

Orville "Porky" Meyers of Lansing, Iowa, and Harry "Ponce" DeLeon of Moline, Illinois, were two motor canoe specialists who gained considerable fame hunting and fishing every nook and cranny of the Mississippi River, from Muscatine to Dubuque using a modified 17-foot Grumman square stern with a 10-horse Johnson. They cut a V-shaped plate out of 3/8 inch aluminum and riveted it to the canoe keel under the stern. The wings of the "V" extended beyond the motor shaft, causing the stern, under power, to remain level. Thus the canoe skimmed the surface at high speed. Not only did this combination fairly fly over the water at a teeth-chattering 25 mph, but when Porky and Ponce wished to cross a river sandbar, they simply hit the bar wide open, jerked the motor upright, and jumped across. The one ride I had with these daredevils was sufficient and I do not advocate this exercise in any way; but these two canoemen knew exactly what they were doing and covered a lot of hunting and fishing territory in this manner.

A big motor, beside making a canoe stern-heavy and difficult to maneuver, tends to drag the canoe down if it swamps. There are no published floatation comparisons on motor sizes with swamped canoes, but it makes sense that a canoe with a light two-horse will not sink as fast as one with a heavier six. Our preference is a 2 horse which gets something like 20 miles on a gallon of gas and is light enough we can pick it up with one hand.

Old style square sterns are flat in the back, squat and bummers to paddle. The "T" sterns are easier to paddle but not as easy to maneuver under power. On trips where there is also considerable paddling, we prefer a detachable side mount on our light double-end paddle canoe.

Motor canoes are handy for getting to more distant fishing and hunting areas quickly and for moving heavy loads. In stiff headwinds, the motor allows the canoeists to concentrate on seamanship without the fatigue of swinging a paddle all day. This is an important point with a solo traveler who can cover water he could never navigate by arm power. However, motor canoes are not foolproof in rough water. It takes as much skill to handle a power canoe in heavy waves as it does with a paddle craft and if the motor quits, it's prayer time. Side bracket motors tend to throw water over the stern in a heavy sea and they steer somewhat differently since they are located alongside the stern seat and have a pivoting effect at that point. They do not respond quickly when the canoe needs to be turned.

In river currents, outboards sometimes do weird things on canoes. When heading upstream, turbulence may tend to jerk the motor from side to side. It pays to have an alert bowman with a paddle handy when climbing around sunken rocks to fend off contact. Hitting rock solidly with a motor usually means a sheared pin and being immediately at the mercy of the current. Going downstream in turbulence, we usually shut off the motor and use our paddles for better control.

Sometimes we use a single motor between two canoes lashed together with poles attached to the thwarts. We space our canoes three feet apart with a slight-toe in to reduce slop which tends to come up between the two hulls. This will work with two paddle canoes, one with a side bracket, or with a square stern and a paddle canoe although in that instance, the rear pole needs to be lashed from the center thwart of the square stern on an angle back to the stern thwart of the paddle craft.

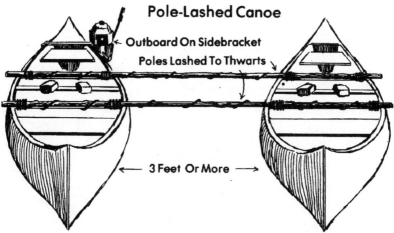

Pole-Lashed Canoe

Outboard On Sidebracket

Poles Lashed To Thwarts

← 3 Feet Or More →

Another common method of using two canoes and one motor is to tow one behind the other. We tie the tow rope to the leading motor canoe but have the bow paddler in the trailing craft tie the rope to the spare paddle and brace it against the bow piece. This way, if there is difficulty, the bow man can simply flip the paddle overboard, freeing the two canoes. It also helps if the stern paddler in the towed craft uses his paddle as a rudder to keep the two canoes directly in line.

We use a side-by-side rig with poles when sailing two canoes downwind. This is handy when traveling across large lakes and can save a lot of arm effort. Four poles are lashed to form a frame for the tarp "sail," secured on all sides. The bottom pole "boom" rests across the gunwales and the top pole is held in place by ropes at the comers. If the wind becomes too strong, or for some reason progress needs to cease, the ropes can be slacked off and the sail lowered.

A word of caution about side-lashed canoes: They are initially quite stable, like a pontoon boat. But in rough water they are not as seaworthy together as the two canoes separate and can give the canoeists a false sense of security. They are not much good at all in whitewater. As a platform for casting, they are excellent, even

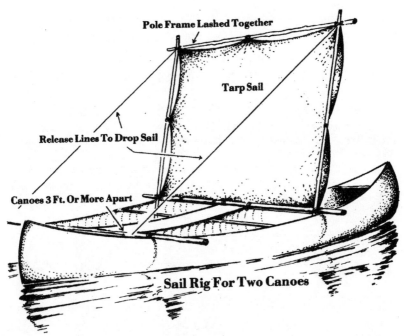

Pole Frame Lashed Together

Tarp Sail

Release Lines To Drop Sail

Canoes 3 Ft. Or More Apart

Sail Rig For Two Canoes

allowing anglers to stand up. But caution must be taken if four people are fishing from lashed canoes to make sure somebody's ear doesn't get perforated by a backcast.

When traveling any distance with side-by-side craft, we lash the poles with a single rope, using half hitches to the thwarts from gunwale to gunwale. Tied off with a quick release knot, it is easy to break down the lashings at portages.

Guides assert that a motor is only as good as the tool kit. Trouble should be anticipated and maintenance requires tools. Any canoe-ist who motors into the bush without at least a nodding acquaintance with his power plant is likely to return by paddle only.

Trouble may occur with either the motor or the fuel on about a 50-50 basis. Fuel should be mixed fresh in clean, tightly-capped containers. Plastic gas cans come with a nozzle for filling motors, but a fine-meshed screened funnel is indispensable for keeping bits of dirt or drops of water out of the motor tank. Metal funnels do not float so we fasten ours with a piece of line to the gas can handle.

Water in the gas may become apparent immediately since the

64

water will sink to the bottom of the tank and gets into the fuel line at once. A drop or two of water may go right through a hot motor with maybe a cough or two, but more than that will stop a motor cold. Water in can or tank may sometimes be spotted with a flashlight. It looks like a flat bubble rolling around on the bottom. If gas is in short supply, the "good" gas may be poured slowly off the top of the contaminated can through a screened funnel into a clean container and the watery residue dumped on the rocks to evaporate.

There may come an occasion when a motor canoe swamps. If the motor is running, water may be sucked up inside the cylinders and the motor will need be uncapped, the fuel dumped out, the tank and carburetor completely emptied. Then some raw gas can be sloshed into the cylinders, swished around and dumped out. Similarly, raw gas is flushed through the carburetor and out the drain hole. All the gas in the gas tank is dumped out and the spark plug removed and dried. Then the motor is allowed to dry out in the air for a time, refueled and started up.

Our tool kit contains a spark plug wrench, pliers, adjustable wrench, screw driver, extra spark plugs, shear pins and an extra cotter pin taped to the motor handle, a piece of emery cloth for cleaning plugs, a coil of wire and a roll of tape.

Prior to each trip, the motor should be tuned. Every north country outfitter has seen canoeists load up at the dock, gas their outboard, set the choke, then pull the starter cord and pull and pull. And a whole lot of pulls. This is usually accompanied by the comment: "Well, it was running OK when we put it away last fall." Uh huh.

If something goes wrong with one cylinder on a two-cylinder motor there will be a distinct drop in power. The bad plug can be removed and the motor started up again. With a one-cylinder motor, it simply stops. It takes only a moment to remove the spark plug and put in a new one. Old plugs can be cleaned up and put in the tool kit for spares.

Sometimes the recoil spring in the starter will snap. In this case, the cowl is unscrewed, the rewind removed, stuffed in a pack and the motor started manually with a rope. If a motor "freezes up" it is usually because somebody didn't mix any oil in the gas. Stuck pistons can usually be loosened after they cool by removing the spark plugs, pouring a little raw gas into the cylinders and tapping the top of each piston with a hardwood stick through the spark plug hole, alternately pulling on the starter cord. Once the pistons are loose, gas up with the proper fuel mixture and the motor will usually run all right.

Another trouble sign is a grinding sound with a jerking on the shaft, an indication that the lower gear box may have no gear oil. It is essential when starting a trip to check the lower unit, fill it with oil and make sure the oil plugs are in tight. One very common method of accidentally de-greasing the lower unit is by getting monofilament line wrapped in the prop. This can easily occur when trolling if the canoe runs over the line. In that case, the nylon will bunch between the prop and the soft brass grease seal, chew through the seal and allow the grease to escape. When the grease goes out of the lower unit, the gears stick and the trip becomes a paddle-only activity.

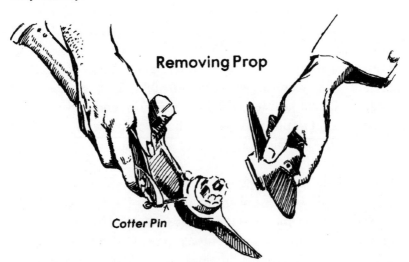

Removing Prop

Cotter Pin

A broken shear pin is indicated when the motor hits something and begins to race with no forward progress. Most motors are equipped with a clutch arrangement so that when an underwater obstacle hits the prop, the prop disengages rather than knocking off the blade. The soft brass shear pin is located in a slot on the prop shaft. It will break with a hard hit, freeing the prop and drive shaft from more extensive damage. The cotter pin is removed, the motor prop cap unscrewed, the broken shear pin taken out and a new one inserted. Reassembled, the motor can be started up and the trip resumed.

During any motor repair, the canoe should be beached. Repairs should be handled on dry land, over a poncho or a tarp so any pieces dropped will not be lost. Attempting to repair a motor on the water may result in some essential part being dropped into the lake.

The last major problem with an outboard and one that may sound ridiculous, is losing the motor altogether. It happens often enough. Every motor is equipped with one or two hand screws used to fasten it to the transom or side bracket. If the screws are not on tight, the motor may jump off the mount and disappear. A chain or piece of rope connecting the motor to the canoe is good insurance and re-checking the screws periodically is a good idea.

Twice I have had motors come off the mounts while under way. One was a 3 -horse that went off a square stern on a sharp turn. It was roped to the transom, but I didn't want it to go into the lake, so I yanked it up onto my lap where it screamed like a banshee until I managed to shut it off. The other was a little 1.5 hsp motor that came off a side mount. I managed to hold onto the steering handle while I cut the spark with my other hand. Both times, my wife commented that this was a novel way to liven up an otherwise uneventful day.

Chapter Thirteen

STAYING UNLOST

It was after supper and a bunch of the guides were sitting around Billy Zup's fishing camp talking about duck hunting when somebody brought up the time Stanley Owl went out in the middle of the night, located a couple of duck hunters lost up on the Bear Trap River and brought them back to camp. "Hey, Stan," somebody asked. "How'd you ever find those guys in the dark?"

"I knew where they got off the trail ... figured they would build a fire and wait for help. They did."

"You never carry a compass, do you, Stan?"

Stanley looked thoughtful for a moment. "Indian doesn't need a compass," he answered matter-of-fact. "Indian always knows where he is."

The guides digested this. Then somebody asked: "You ever been lost, Stan?"

"Nope." His mahogany face split open with a wide grin. "Sometimes camp lost Sometimes canoe lost; but not Stan." He pointed down at his boots. "Stanley is right here."

And that is the literal truth. If you can see your two feet, you are right there. But darn few of us have an infallible sense of direction and none of us care to spend a day or a week in a canoe trying to figure out where we are. That's why we carry a map and a compass and have the knowhow to use both.

68

In some books about wilderness canoe travel, one often runs across the statement: "Traveling with a map and compass is simple." If that were so there wouldn't be so many books and pamphlets trying to tell how simple it is. Outside of Stanley Owl, I can't think of a single guide I know who hasn't admitted getting messed up a few times on directions, sometimes just by reading the map wrong. The tools and methods for charting and following a course on a map are nearly foolproof. It's just that the Lord never saw fit to make human beings foolproof. But we can work at cutting our errors to a minimum.

Anyone who is a map sharpy can simply skip this part of this book. Or if you have no intention on going into wilderness country to pursue fish and game. But in case your knowledge is limited, what follows may be of some help. Fortunately, all of the North American canoe country is mapped. You may find a few funny things on some of the maps like a rapids that is more of a waterfall or a narrow spot in a river that is really a rapids, but mainly the maps are accurate. Topographic maps show the water courses, elevations and some of the portages. But one problem is that maps come in different scales. The most common maps have four miles of terrain condensed to an inch of paper (1:250,000). But you'll also find maps drawn to larger scales like one mile to the inch (1:62,500), one mile to 1 1/4 inches (1:50,000) or one mile to 2 1/2 inches (1:24,000). It is obviously easier to read details on the larger scales, but they are also bulkier. On most trips we have one set of small scale maps (1:250,000) for each canoe and one set of larger scale maps for the group. Care must be taken to make the mental shift switching from a map of one scale to a map of another, say from four miles to the inch to one mile to the inch.

All maps carry legends with symbols, words or both indicating important features of the terrain. They are listed on the map margin for reference. Rapids are marked with a line across the stream, the letter "R", the word "Rapids" or lines running parallel to the stream. Falls may be a line with an "F"' the word "Falls" or a line across two points aiming downstream. A portage may be marked "P" or "por" or just be shown as a dotted line around the rapids.

Lake elevations are usually printed on the main lakes and give an idea of uphill, downhill between lakes.

Brown contour lines show the land elevations. These vary with the scale. On a 1:62,500 map, the lines will show intervals of 20 feet. On a 1:250,000 map, it will be 100 feet. Since the map shows a view from overhead and since the canoeist is on the water level, it takes a little practice to convert one point of view to the other. Along wilderness streams, contours can be a matter of life or death. The system used by most experienced canoeists in unfamiliar wilderness country is to make a "profile" of the stream well in advance of the trip as a means of determining if the route is navigable or not.

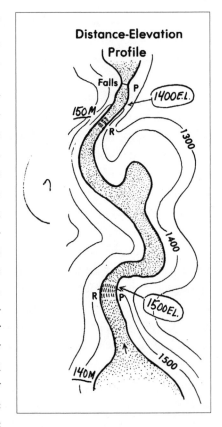

We were taught to use a magnifying glass to follow the stream on the map, marking the elevations at each point where a contour line crosses. Then, using one of those little mileage wheels sold where maps or surveyor's supplies are available, we mark off every 10 miles of river course with the accumulated mileage from the starting point. If we can't locate a wheel, we mark 2 1/2 inches on a piece of string or fish line (2 1/2inches on the four-miles-to-the-inch scale is 10 miles, right?). We lay that piece of string along the stream and mark each 10-mile interval with a pen or pencil.

Now we have our distances for reference on the map and we also have the amount of drop for every 10 miles of river. If that drop runs four to eight feet, it will probably be OK, but if it gets to 10 feet or more per mile, it may be very treacherous. Where several contour lines crowd down to a narrow stretch, it indicates a canyon and if there is considerable drop it could show a disaster area with no way to portage out.

Some people hunt for such challenges and they are welcome to them. If I detect considerable risk to my canoe, outfit, or my epidermis, I aint going and I don't care how good the fishing may be in that stretch.

In any downhill situation, care must be taken to locate takeout points long before the canoe gets into treacherous water. Spring high water is particularly hairy. Few things are more terrifying than to get swept into a roaring chute with no idea what lies below. Some outfitters we know map their customers upstream. This mean a little more work; but the paddlers see every obstacle ahead clearly and won't go sailing into trouble.

Where a decision is made to perhaps "run" a rapids, careful paddlers will always beach their canoe at the top and walk along the river course, "reading" the waters, noting fast rips, boulders, eddies and other features, in effect planning the trip down before it is begun.

Even following a slow, meandering river downstream can have its own problems. Where the river widens out into an island-filled grassy flat, or where it enters a large, irregular lake, the canoeist needs to know something about picking a route with the map, and probably the compass, too.

Let's say we are coming out of Crowrock Bay on Otukamamoan Lake, Ontario, heading for the Trout River and the portage into Redgut Bay of Rainy Lake. We have a Mine Center, Rainy River District, Ontario, map laid out on top of a packsack facing the same direction we are traveling. There is just one gap in the wooded shoreline ahead, marked on the map with three little dots of islands (A). As we paddle past there, we note the long bay to our right (B) and then, hanging to the right shore, we cross the "W" shaped point and paddle between the point and the island (C). This looks something like that last bay we crossed because we are looking right at the trees on the shore ahead, which seem to indicate a dead end. But the map shows a channel out of view behind

71

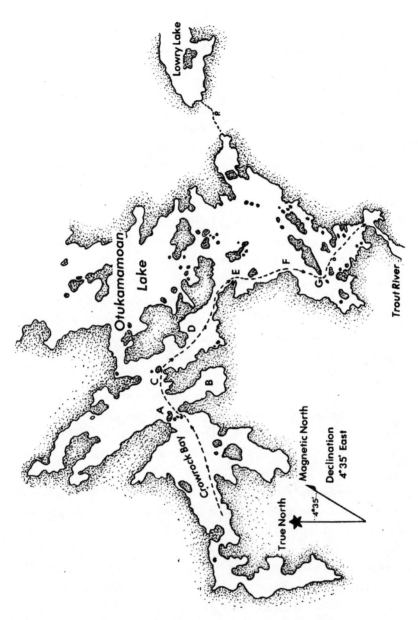

Lowry Lake

Otukamamoan Lake

Trout River

E

F

G

D

C

B

A

Crowrock Bay

True North

Magnetic North

Declination 4°35' East

4°35'

that jutting point (D). So we push on and round the point. Sure enough, there's our channel with some open water and islands beyond. In a half hour, we come out of the channel and pause by the point (E) which is recognizable by a tiny slot in its nose From here we see nothing but a whole lot of irregular shoreline and what

72

looks like bays; but our map tells us it is a bunch of islands and beyond the biggest island lies the river. We figure our best bet is to keep along that right shoreline another mile to the rounded point (F), from where we are able to make out the tip (G) of the big island so that's how we play it.

When we paddle around the tip we see that small, elongated island ahead which looks like a projection of the shore. Our map shows that a line from where we are, across the end of that island and the little oval island behind will hit the mouth of the river. With a feeling of success, we curve down into the channel to the portage.

Notice that we had no need for the compass. We went from a known point and carefully followed landmarks to arrive at our destination. That's how most canoe travel is done. But now let's go to a situation where we will need to "shoot" a compass line.

We're coming down Manitoba's Gammon River into Aiken Lake. The lake is full of islands and weedy bays. We want to cut right across the lake and hit the river leading out and we don't want to waste time picking our way around points and islands. We are using a plastic based Silva Compass with a movable dial. We lay the map flat and place the compass on top, ignoring the wavering magnetic needle for now. With the compass direction arrow pointing the way we want to go, we draw a line along the base plate from our known position (A) to the north tip of the big island (B) which lies directly in front of the river mouth. That island will be our reference point. When we reach there the river is right behind it.

With the base plate lying along our route line, we rotate the compass dial so the letter "N" is up and one of the meridian lines inside the dial coincides with a meridian line on the map. The top of the map is north. The "N" on the compass is north. We have both aligned. Now we look to where it says "Read bearing here" and we see the number 290. That is the true geographic bearing from where we are to the point on that distant island; but it isn't the compass bearing. The compass bearing is a magnetic bearing because the needle points to magnetic north, not map or "true"

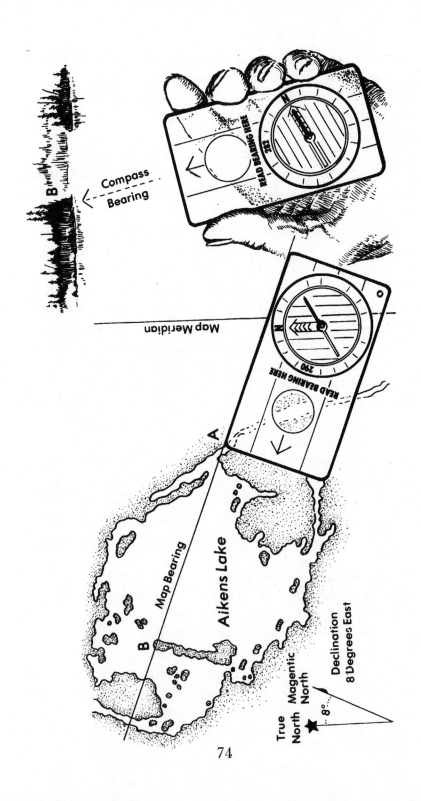

Compass Bearing

Map Meridian

READ BEARING HERE 282

READ BEARING HERE 290

A

B

Map Bearing

Aikens Lake

True North

Magentic North

Declination 8 Degrees East

8°

74

north. And that is why all this business is not so simple. There are really two norths: One is "true north" or geographic north at the North Pole at the top of the world where all the map meridian lines converge. But the magnetic lines and our compass converge at the magnetic pole which moves around a little every year, but is currently at Bathurst Island in the Arctic about 1,000 miles south of the geographic North Pole. Every compass in working order will have its needle pointing to magnetic north (unless we do something silly like getting a steel knife blade or metal fishing reel too close which throws the needle off).

The difference between true or map north and magnetic north is called the "declination." It is printed in the margin of the map as a V-shaped symbol with the number of degrees east or west.

If we happened to be heading on a trip north from the Grand Portage, Minnesota, Indian Reservation, we have no concern with that declination because at that point, magnetic north and true north are in the same line. This is why map travel over most of the Boundary Waters is so easy. Both magnetic north and true north are just about the same; but when we move east or west the situation changes. For instance, a canoeist in northern Maine will find that his map shows a declination of about 18 degrees west. That is, the compass needle will be pointing 18 degrees west of north. And the farther north a person goes, the greater it becomes. In northern Alaska, the compass needle will be pointing northeast because that is where the north magnetic pole is in relation to Alaska. If we somehow got to Ellef Ringness Island in the Arctic (heaven forbid) we would discover that magnetic "north" on our compass is now straight south!

But enough of that. Our map shows that the declination at Aikens Lake is 8 degrees east. This means that the compass needle is pointing 8 degrees farther to the right of true north. So we have to subtract 8 degrees in order to get our compass bearing the same as the map. Eight from 290 is 282, which is our magnetic bearing and which is what we will be traveling. We rotate the dial to a bearing of 282 and with the compass flat we turn it until the magnetic needle lines up with "N" on the map. Now we sight down the arrow that says "Read Bearing Here" and that arrow will be pointing across the lake to the tip of the island. If we can see clearly enough, we can pick out a big pine or a clump of spruce and paddle toward it. If we can't see across the lake (if there is heavy fog or it is dark) we can simply lay the compass on the bottom of the canoe parallel to the keel line and paddle ahead keeping the canoe aimed at the bearing of 282. We will come out pretty close to the tip of the island. From there we paddle across to the right-hand shore and follow it around the corner to the river. (Just a mile and a half ahead is a campsite and we may have time to get a few walleyes for supper.)

Sometimes we don't use a Silva compass. Sometimes we carry a military "lensatic" compass that doesn't have a rotating dial. To make things easy, we carry a little plastic protractor in our map case and here's how it works with our Gammon Lake map. Where our bearing line intersects with the north-south meridian, we center the protractor. We see that the number of degrees between the two lines is 70. That is, our bearing is 70 degrees west of north which on our compass is 290. OK, we subtract that 8 degree east declination and have our magnetic bearing of 282. Holding the compass level, we bring it up to our eye, turning it slowly until 282 shows up clearly in the eyepiece of the lens. The top of the lens is slotted like a rear rifle sight. The cover has a thin wire fixed dead center. We line up the wire with the slot and look across the lake, getting a fix on a clump of spruce we determine is on the end of the island. We fold up the map, put away the compass and paddle to that clump of spruce, go around the tip of the island, head to the right hand shore and follow that to the mouth of the Gammon river.

It becomes readily apparent that to follow any map course, with or without a compass, we must keep an accurate record of where we started and what reference points we pass. We can do this with a pencil or in our heads, but we must keep track of where we are in relation to the terrain and on the map.

But let's suppose we didn't. Let's suppose on the first lake, Otukamamoan, we went straight across the lake instead of south, paddled into the bay going toward Lowry Lake, thinking it was the mouth of the Trout River, and wound up in a dead end. Yikes! Of course we can paddle back out of that bay but now all the water and all the islands start to look alike. Our first order of business is to get the map and the lake together which means we've got to get the map pointed north so we can make sense out of all the points and islands around us. North on the map is a bearing of 360 degrees. On Otukamamoan Lake, the variation is just 4 degrees east. OK we lay our Silva compass on the map with the bearing arrow "N" and the dial meridian lines in line with one of the north-south map meridians. Then we turn the whole works until the magnetic needle points at 4 degrees. Oh, so now we are adding 4 degrees. When we go from the map to the magnetic bearing; and the variation is east, we subtract. So when we go from the magnetic bearing back to the map, we add.

Now we have the map right with the lake. But where the heck are we? We can look back at that lousy dead-end bay. It runs east-west. Yeah, and right in the entrance is kind of a square-looking island. So now we hunt around the map. Ahah! Behold and lo, there is our bay, square island and all. And we start to laugh. For the love of Pete, instead of going south, we paddled east right across the lake. Well, sure. There to the south is that bunch of islands and all we have to do now is pick our way through them to the mouth of the Trout River. But we won't pull any more klutzy tricks like losing track of where we are. No sir.

Map and compass reading is simple? Like fun. And we should be darn good at it before we travel to heck and gone out into the boonies. We must memorize the rule on declinations: when going from map to compass bearing - subtract for east, add for west. And we must remember the reverse is true when we go from compass bearing back to the map. We don't have to be on the water to practice map work, either. We can get a map of the local area park, farmland, anywhere on dry land. We can start from a known point and plot a course to another point, correct for the variation and walk the compass bearing to see if we come out where we are supposed to.

77

Every state department of conservation and every Canadian provincial ministry of Lands and Forests has maps of its lakes and streams. A good source in Canada is the Canada Map Office, 615 Booth St., Ottawa, Ontario KIA OE9. That same office has detailed aerial maps of most wilderness areas Also the Canadian National Railways are an excellent source of information on trips that can be made by loading canoes and equipment into a freight car and going by rail to remote areas.

Topographic maps in the U.S. are available from the U.S. Geological Survey, 1200 S. Eads St., Arlington, VA 22202 for areas east of the Mississippi River and from the U.S. Geological Survey, Federal Center, Denver, CO 80225 for the west. U.S. Corps of Engineers offices in most major cities have detailed maps of rivers and lakes, but they don't show all the portages. Maps obtainable from north country canoe outfitters do and also show the location of campsites in many areas.

It is advisable to learn navigational skills in well-traveled areas before heading into the back country, keeping track of the route, checking and re-checking the terrain and direction as if one's life depends on it.

Which it ultimately does.

Chapter 14
REPAIRS ON THE TRAIL

The late afternoon sun was just beginning to nudge its way into the wedge of birch and balsam that flank Jasper Creek to the west of our outfitting base on Moose Lake. The metallic thump of canoe hulls at the dock indicated that a man we'll call "Eddie," his wife and two sons had paddled in from their trip. In a few moments, they trudged up the gravel path to the lodge and dropped their Duluth packs on the shaded porch.

"How'd it go?" we asked.

"Had a good trip," Eddie replied. "Well, up to today. We had a little problem coming in today and a hole got cut in the canoe."

There is no word that freezes the arteries of an outfitter more quickly than the word "hole."

"Not in that new 15-footer?" I asked with growing apprehension.

"Yeah, I'm afraid it was," Eddie admitted. "But we got it fixed and paddled in OK."

At that point one of our guides, Mike Banovetz, came up from the dock area where he had been working on outboard motors. "Better take a look at that new Grumman," he murmured. "It's got more than just a cut."

79

The 15-footer, a lightweight on its maiden trip, was tied alongside the dock. That is, the bow section was tied to the dock. The stern half angled off toward the middle of the lake at an angle of about 10 degrees. It was readily apparent that the canoe had gone sideways down a rapids, went between two rocks and had broken at the middle thwart. The left gunwale had been ripped apart, the right one bent and the right section of the hull had acquired a couple of accordion pleats. Eddie and his boys had obviously pushed and pounded the bent aluminum back into some semblance of shape and then sealed the rips with a couple rolls of plumber's duct tape. The fact that they paddled that crooked hull back to the base was something to marvel at. But I didn't marvel very long.

Eddie paid for the canoe. That is, he paid for the replacement. Canoe outfitters usually take dents and small cuts in stride but a structural break puts the watercraft out of the rental business. Eddie became the owner of a 15-foot wreck which we strapped to the roof of his car for the 600-mile trip home to Chicago. I suggested that he locate an aluminum welder in that area who could straighten and weld the hull so it would be serviceable. Which he subsequently did, providing a paddle craft for his family to enjoy on northern Illinois rivers.

Before he left for home, however, he was more than a little irritated about having to replace the canoe. On the other hand, his wife was grinning, taking it all in stride.

"You're accepting it pretty well," I said to her when Eddie was out of earshot.

"It's really funny," she said. "We had already portaged around that rapids but Eddie insisted the boys carry the canoe back up and paddle down so he could get it on our video camera. The boys were tired and didn't want to go, but Eddie insisted. They carried the canoe back up to the top of the rapids, put it in, swamped and the canoe broke so we wind up with a wreck and a $250 film sequence."

There is no particular moral to this story other than that they had taken some duct tape along in their duffle for an emergency.

80

The emergency occurred and they managed to get back.

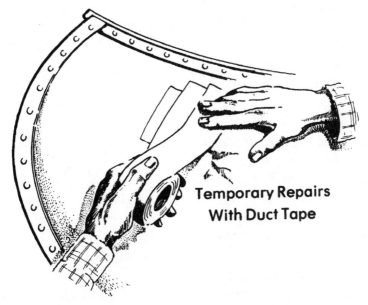

**Temporary Repairs
With Duct Tape**

The voyageurs of fur trade history were forever repairing their birchbark craft, a daily chore when camp was made for the night. Small cuts, cracks or rips were patched with pitch - a quantity of spruce gum scraped from trees, heated and mixed with a small amount of grease used to create a black, plastic-like gum. More extensive repairs to bark canoes might involve sewing a torn seam or lacing a loose gunwale with thin strands of spruce root, even replacing a cracked rib or fractured cedar planking, new members carved out of the forest, wedged or laced in place.

There are a lot of us who, in an emergency, have resorted to pitch to plug a hole or a seam in an aluminum or plastic canoe, but pitch is awful gummy and there are other, less messy means available. Duct tape is the universal emergency repair item, but does not necessarily cover every situation which may arise, particularly in a wilderness trip of some length.

Every canoeist, no matter how skilled, plans for possible damage and repairs. The best plan is to avoid trouble. Significantly, the voyageurs and Native Americans did not do dumb things when traveling, like running bad rapids. There is considerable mythology about the old timers running down foamy rapids in a bark canoe, but they simply didn't. First, they were too darn smart to risk wrecking their means of transportation. Secondly, in regard to the voyageurs, they were either hauling in loads of valuable trade goods or hauling out a whole winter's catch of furs and they were not about to risk any of that for whitewater thrills. They either portaged around the rapids or carefully "snubbed" down. For that exercise, each canoeman carried a long pole. Going down through whitewater, they dropped their paddles and grabbed the poles. As the canoe moved into the fast current, they jammed the poles down against the bottom, holding the canoe to a slow descent. A few poles at a time were pulled up and shoved forward, allowing the loaded canoe to ride slowly down under control. As poles were lifted and then jammed back down, the canoe edged safely down the current until it hit flat water where the voyageurs lay down their poles and took off paddling again.

Every canoe camping kit should contain items which can be used to mend canoes, paddles, packs, tents, clothing and sleeping bags. This does not require a lot of stuff, just some essentials that will fit in the flap of a packsack.

The most frequently damaged item is the canoe. Temporary repairs of cuts can be handled on just about any hull with duct tape - the two-inch stuff. It will stick to nearly anything, is extremely tough and fairly impervious to water. Aluminum canoes are fairly easy to mend, even severely damaged ones. It is seldom a section of hull is completely knocked out. The metal will tear or bend, but will usually hang together. We have used a couple of smooth rocks, like the hammers used by body and fender men on cars - one rock against the metal inside, the other pounded on the out-side to smooth out a tear. Once the damage is pounded out, it can be taped over and the trip resumed.

Liquid metal that comes in tubes can help patch small leaks in aluminum canoes. To improve sticking, the wound is dried and sandpapered back an inch or so to remove grime. Liquid metal is not much good for repairing large cuts or holes and it is not easy to remove later at home where more extensive repairs can be attempted. But it will work on small problems.

On some aluminum canoes, such as Grummans, bulkheads were fastened in with small bolts and nuts. These have a tendency to loosen from vibration. It takes a Phillips screwdriver to tighten the screw and a pliers to anchor the nut inside. Those same bulkhead bolts are where contact is made with bottom rocks. The recurring impact may grind off the aluminum next to the bolt to create an outside leak. Cracks like these and similar small leaks along the keel are difficult to spot with the naked eye. If the canoe is propped right side up on a couple of logs and filled with several buckets of water, the leaks can usually be detected. Tape doesn't work too well on bulkhead bolts in rocky streams because the rocks keep ripping the tape loose. Liquid metal works best here.

Bolts and screws in the yoke pads can work loose and it pays to inspect these from time to time. If a yoke pad comes loose, the pad can be squeezed down and wrapped in place with duct tape.

A pocket repair kit for an aluminum canoe may contain small screwdrivers (Phillips and regular), a few extra bulkhead and thwart bolts, sandpaper, a roll of duct tape and a tube of liquid metal.

Wood and canvas canoes can be cut or punctured but are not difficult to fix. A repair kit should include that handy roll of duct tape, a tube of waterproof glue, some canvas, sandpaper, copper wire, a square of thin copper sheeting, and copper tacks. Small cuts can be covered with tape sealed with the glue. More extensive repairs may require the damaged area to be sanded back a bit and a piece of canvas cut an inch or so larger than the hole. This can be covered with glue and slipped into the hole against the planking and smoothed out. A top patch can be glued over the hole and the under patch. If fairly large, it can be held in place with copper tacks.

A hole punched clear through the canvas and planking may be repaired by gluing the splintered edges and pushing the wood back into place. A piece of sheet copper may be cut to fit between the ribs inside and locked in place with glue and tacks Then the injury can be covered with canvas glued to the outside. The whole works can be sanded smooth later and painted over with scarcely a blemish.

A fiber glass or Kevlar canoe may be patched up on the trail with duct tape and more extensive repairs completed at home.

Broken paddles are a common ailment and an extra is usually packed along. Most often it is the paddle shaft that breaks, somewhere above the blade. There are books that will tell a person how to hack a new paddle out of a piece of log, but repairing the old one is usually simpler. To fix a broken shaft, saw or whittle both parts of the break at an angle and sand them smooth. Then the two pieces of the shaft may be glued and wrapped with cord or fish line. Paddle breaks occur for several reasons, one being that the paddler has his lower hand too far away from the throat

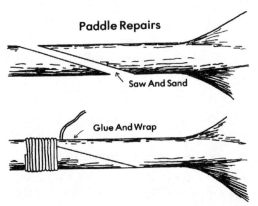

Paddle Repairs

Saw And Sand

Glue And Wrap

of the paddle. This puts stress on the most vulnerable part of the paddle - the shaft. It is almost impossible to break a paddle with one hand on the cap and one down tight to the throat. Another method of breaking a paddle consists of using it for a pry bar or a pole, shoving it against the bottom of the lake or stream.

Next to canoes and paddles, tents are most easily damaged. These include cuts, punctures and burn holes, abrasions, torn seams and peg loops or guy tabs. Tape will usually make sufficient temporary repairs. Pulled seams and ripped off loops need to be sewn, which requires a needle and thread. In an emergency, a piece of boot lace can be used as a peg or rope loop.

Probably zippers cause more problems on tents than anything else. A common ailment is a gap opening up after the door has been zipped shut. This may be caused by dirt or by a worn zipper slide. A zipper can be cleaned by unzipping it all the way and brushing the zipper teeth with a tooth brush. Sometimes, pinching both sides of the slide with pliers will make it perform better. A totally wrecked zipper can be replaced in an emergency with a row of safety pins. In our camping repair kit we have four needles - two large and two small - a couple different spools of thread, a thimble and a dozen safety pins. These can be used to repair shirts and pants as well as tents.

Like everything else, it is better to have well-maintained gear and clothing and to avoid rips and cuts. Duct tape can also be used to seal damage to shirts, pants and rain gear, but it is not particularly neat looking.

Chapter Fifteen

WHAT'S WITH A FISHING GUIDE?

It is quite easy for a quartet of anglers to spend $2,000 or more each on a wilderness fishing trip, tallying in accommodations, outfitting, travel (perhaps including float plane service) to be located in what should be a fisherman's paradise, which may or may not be the case. One acid test for the chance of success at any resort, is a quick check of the fish cleaning shack. A roomy, clean, tightly screened facility that smells like fish usually indicates a fair amount of traffic. A dilapidated, dusty, ill-equipped shack that shows little use may very well indicate that the lake whereon the resort is located may be deficient in the raw material for a fish fry. On an extended wilderness canoe trip, of course, there is no fish cleaning shack.

Contrary to some impressions, there really are fish in most lakes and rivers. But where? Bait and tackle shops often have tidbits of information and, perhaps, maps. With the advent of portable electronic devices and good depth charts, a canoe angler with fair skill may very well connect. Electronic devices are considered by some as just one more encumbrance and hardly worth the trouble. It's a toss up. There is certainly some satisfaction in prospecting new territory and finding the piscatorial mother lode. There is also the possibility of finding few or no fish.

A guide can be the key to success and his fee is usually money well spent. No matter how skilled an angler, it is difficult to surpass a veteran guide in his own territory. A couple of days or a week with a guide can put fishermen in places they might likely never discover. It is a guide's business to find fish and most are quite knowledgeable. While some guides handle both canoe and boat customers, canoe guides are often specialists with distinct skills.

One way to establish relations is for the sportsman to show interest in catch-and-release, noting that perhaps just a photo of the odd trophy will do and maybe a fish dinner or two. He can point out that he is not interested in depopulating the guide's favorite spots. Indeed, many camps and guides advertise just such rules of operation.

Many of the most skillful professional anglers seek the services of guides. The years I operated a canoe outfitting base on the rim of the 4,000-square-mile Quetico-Superior wilderness, I had a staff of excellent guides who were in constant demand. Some of their clients were fishing pros. The guide's value was not only for locating fish, but also for knowing the best campsites, erecting a snug camp, paddling and cooking. But knowledge of the fish was uppermost.

Guides who are on the waters, week in and week out, are good at keeping tabs on where the fish are currently located and what they are taking. In case of abrupt weather changes, they are quickest to observe and adjust to the shift. With a 15 degree drop in temperature, fish found in six feet of water today may be in 25 tomorrow. At some seasons, the fish may be inshore; at another, out on remote reefs. Guides have all this in their play book.

If possible, it is well to hire a guide well ahead of the trip. Usually, the best guides are booked early. Some, such as the legendary Harry and Mary Lambirth, operating out of Ely, Minnesota, are booked solid two years in advance. Most of the top guides are expert in all disciplines, which may include spinning, bait casting, fly casting or live bait angling. And they may have suggestions as to the best times of season and preferred tackle. Experienced guides readily furnish references along with their rates; but such guides do not come cheap. Occasionally, one may locate a rather inexpensive, part time guide who proves excellent as a fish finder. And sometimes high school kids who grew up in a specific area and belonged to a dedicated fishing family can prove exceedingly helpful at a moderate price But these are most often exceptions.

Not only does an experienced guide pinpoint the fish, but he also frees up the fisherman from paddling so he can concentrate on fishing. On trout streams, this can be an essential part of the expedition because the guide will know exactly what is coming up, where to place and hold the canoe so the angler gets a maximum shot at the best spots. He will also know what stretches may be relatively fishless and may be ignored.

Guides we have known were all individuals and, to some extent, specialists. We played by their rules and didn't try to override them. If success is not forthcoming after a time, a skilled angler may find it worthwhile to offer some suggestions or at least engage the guide in discussing what other possibilities might be effective. Once on a remote small lake on Vancouver Island, we were in the midst of a significant rise of cutthroat trout although our success rate was not eye-popping. The guide advocated use of a Cowitchan Special, a fly with which he had had some previous exceptional luck. The cutthroats provided some action on that fly, but not commensurate with the surface activity. It was a windy day and I managed to scoop up some of the insects upon which the trout were feeding-black terrestrials which were being blown into the lake. After a time, I switched to a tiny black panfish popping bug and really sorted out those trout.

"What in the world are you using?" the guide inquired at length. "Black panfish popper." I handed one over to the guide who inspected it thoroughly. In that part of Canada, panfish were not a common species. The guide had never seen a popping bug other than in a catalog. He was sufficiently impressed, however, and gratefully accepted several of the cork-headed lures which he put to good use when the wind was blowing land-based insects into the water.

And once, when lead-headed jigs were first entering the tackle market, we were on an Ontario Lake with a guide who assured us that live bait was the only current means of nailing smallmouth bass. Indeed, live bait was working exceedingly well, but when we switched to jigs with plastic bodies the catch rate increased.

But these were rare instances. In the overwhelming number of cases, the local guide had a firm handle on what was working best and his knowledge was the key to some memorable action. In the spring of 2004, my wife Edie's sister Rosemary and husband Carl visited from Potomac, Maryland. To impress them with north country walleye angling, we obtained the services of veteran guide Steve Kleist who had been experiencing considerable success. Steve announced beforehand that leeches were working exceptionally well so we embarked with two canoes appropriately equipped. Steve took Rosemary and Carl in one canoe, Edie and I set out in the other, planning to meet at a campsite later for a walleye lunch.

The weather had turned cold, but we weren't much concerned until Edie and I found ourselves fishless with lunch fast approaching. We had been using standard jig-and-leech combos, changing to different colored jigs in an attempt to entice the fish. Yet, our luck was scant and our concern heightened by the fact that neither Rosemary nor Carl were experienced at fishing. At noon, we paddled to the shore lunch site, fully expecting Rosemary and Carl to be totally disappointed. To our surprise, they enthusiastically showed us a fine string of fat walleyes which Steve was filleting and

subsequently cooked on a camp stove along with beans and potatoes.

"What were they hitting on?" I asked Steve.

"Leeches," he replied.

"Edith and I were using leeches and jigs but couldn't buy a bite."

"Jigs wouldn't work," Steve confirmed. "We found leeches on
very small plain hooks with Lindy Rigs were the ticket ... fished
slow on the bottom."

It was a case where I didn't follow Steve close enough to get all
the details locked down. He had been fishing that same stretch for
several days and knew what would work and what wouldn't. A
simple shift in tactics by the guide made all the difference. Steve
provided Carl and Rosemary with a memorable experience.

When contacting and engaging a guide, it is well to spell out
exactly what you are looking for. General fishing is one thing, but
if you are specifically interested in trout, walleye or bass, it is best
to lay this out beforehand. It may make a lot of difference when
the guide is mapping out the route.

Guides get all manner of customers who become hot stove top-
ics when guides get together over coffee in the winter. While they
handle all sorts of tourists, they tend to peg them in one of three
classifications: first, and fortunately somewhat rare is the "horse's
patoot," the overbearing know-it-all who sets out to impress the
guide with his skill and kno-
whow. Guides accept this,
pull their hats down tighter
and brace for a long ordeal.
Second, and most common,
are the vast number of pleasant customers simply interested in having a good experience. Last, are the truly
helpful clients who pitch in
on the camp chores, are not
afraid to cut wood or wash
dishes, portage their share

Canoe Trip Tackle

Single Hook Lures

90

and try to learn all they can from the guide. Many professional guides have clients who become close personal friends, coming back year after year and maintaining contact through the off season.

And there are families where the parents brought the kids, the kids grew up and brought the grandkids, wishing them to experience the skills and character of a genuine northwoods canoe guide.

If a client has certain dietary requirements, he should convey this to the guide well ahead of the trip so the menu can be planned accordingly. Also, some people have various afflictions and require medication. It is the client's responsibility, of course, to make sure he has his pills along. But it doesn't hurt to explain any problems to the guide.

Several times, at our canoe outfitting base, we had customers with serious insect allergies. They carried antidotes in the event that they might be stung by a bee or a wasp, a trauma which could have lethal effects. We once had a family in the Quetico, with the father extremely sensitive to insect bites. Coming out on a lakeshore at the end of a portage, he accidentally struck a wasp nest with the bow of his canoe, stirring up an army of angry insects. The guide, directly behind, immediately assessed the situation, dropped his canoe and on the dead run, flipped the canoe off the father, grabbed the man around the waist and shoved him head first into the lake, then went back to deal with the swarm of wasps. A week later, at the end of the trip, the father told me: "The quick thinking of the guide probably saved my life." As well he might.

From the business standpoint, every guide knows that a successful trip means a happy client and probably a substantial tip. Many people strongly recommend certain guides to their friends, an added incentive for doing a good job. Like any other endeavor, the guide business is a business.

Some, like the legendary Bill Magie were accomplished story tellers as much in demand for their entertainment value as other skills. Ray Adams, an Ojibwe from Fort Frances, was one of the strongest packers we ever fished with, but Ray seldom said more than two or three words all day. Most southern guides on the float

91

trip streams in Arkansas and Missouri are colorful yarn spinners as are the Quebecois of the Laurentian Divide, although the client may not understand a lot of French.

Guides realize that people who book fishing and hunting trips into remote country are generally reasonable folk who recognize that there may be inherent factors of hardship and discomfort involved. They do not expect flush toilets and maid service in the bush. Most sincerely respect the natural resources and scenery of the area. In this respect, both client and guide start off on the same foot.

Guides are almost essential for many hunting trips. Some states and Canadian provinces require hunters to acquire the services of a guide before venturing into moose, bear, caribou, elk, sheep and deer country. This is not only to assure the game is properly hunted and handled correctly, but also that the hunters return safely to their point of origin.

Chapter Sixteen
HOME ON THE SHORELINE

A rolling line of greenish-black clouds wiped out the sun and blackened the surface of Manitoba's Nelson River as a tree-bending gale howled through the spruce forest. A dozen Cree women and kids, scattering to the shelter of their cabins on the far shore, were suddenly blotted from view by the driving rain.

There was a momentary gasp, as though the whole outdoors had sucked in its breath. Then the full force of the storm slammed our tent, making the rain fly crackle, yanking the guy ropes and probing to find a line or peg that could be tugged loose or pried up. Luckily, the advance buildup of towering thunderheads and jagged shafts of lightning had given ample warning that a real gully washer was bearing down. Pegs secured, guy lines tight, our nylon shelter swayed with the bending trees but stayed erect.

Inside, my wife had a candle lit, a flickering yellow symbol of defiance that somewhat buoyed our spirits like a thumb to the nose against the fury outside. We arranged our rolled-up sleeping bags into seats, opened the food pack and snacked on sausage, cheese and Rye Crisp. We let the storm blow itself out.

There was a time when a furious thunderstorm was a real cause of concern on the canoe trails. The old canvas wall tents could be uprooted from their moorings or simply blown flat. Care had to be taken not to touch the interior walls or ceilings of "waterproof" canvas lest the air seal be broken and rain pour through. In a driving wind, rain often poured through anyway. If it didn't come through the top, it would run down the sides and come racing across the floor.

Today's tightly woven synthetic fabrics, zippered doorways, waterproof floors and rain fly give no camper a reason to experience discomfort. Canoe fishermen or hunters can now live as comfortable in a lightweight tent as in a small cabin. And new fabrics have allowed for a variety of styles. While there are yet a number of serviceable "A" tents with peak roofs available, a whole new array of dome tents combine roomy interiors with ease of erection and interior self-support.

Locating a tent site in wilderness country is rather simple. The campsites used by Ojibwe and Cree paddlers for centuries are still found along the main water courses. In most cases, these are clearings sited on flat, open points where breezes keep insects at bay and abate summer heat. For hunting, we seek sheltered campsites situated within balsam or spruce thickets, away from the wind and

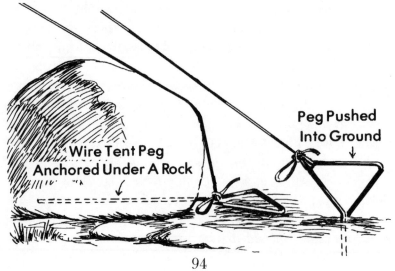

adjacent to ample dry firewood. We avoid picturesque campsites under tall pines, recognizing that those towering white and Norway pines are living lightning rods, attracting dangerous electrical bolts. Sometimes those needled lightning attractors show scars from previous strikes - vertical scorched slashes in the bark. We camp in groves of small trees.

The granite shield country from Minnesota northward has underlying bedrock that is sometimes just inches below the ground surface. It is often difficult to get a tent peg to penetrate far enough to hold the tent. We have found nine-inch wire tent pegs, the ones with triangle-shaped tops, to be the ticket. If the peg cannot be driven in, even at an angle, it can be anchored under a large rock. Tents can also be guyed out with ropes tied to surrounding trees and shrubs. Even if the sun has been shining, we assume a storm can blow up and the tent is anchored accordingly.

Another hazard is a dead or semi-defunct tree hovering over the campsite, a classic "widow maker." Even a camper with an unpracticed eye can spot a leaning tree, awaiting a wind gust to turn it into a tent-crushing deadfall. Nobody has to camp under one of these risks.

Every instruction booklet given out to campers by federal or state forest managers stresses fire location on rock or mineral soil. Yet forest fires annually eat up thousands of acres of our timberlands, many of them started by campers who kindle fires on loose forest duff, dry leaves or pine needles. Folks who have never experienced a forest fire cannot conceive the explosive energy generated when flames hit needles, cones and limbs of conifers. They not only go off like Roman candles, they generate great, airborne balls of fire that go tumbling across the crowns, spreading the conflagration at terrifying speed.

Most cooking fires are kept small and located on solid ground. It takes only a few handfuls of dry sticks to cook a meal. Better yet are the new, lightweight camp stoves like the Dragonfly, which efficiently burn propane. With an insulated shield, heat can be kept inside and whole meals cooked with a minimum of fuel. These stoves are always ready to go and are particularly handy when the weather is rainy and firewood largely soaked. Also, cooking can be done in bad weather with a stove under a nylon kitchen fly without the danger of sparks charring holes in the shelter.

One matter which is not often dealt with in camping books, but vital to any fishing or hunting trip, is the issue of a toilet. Some campers simply back up against a tree, let fly and then kick leaves and duff over the job. Such crude activity in no way improves a campsite and wild critters often uncover such shallow deposits making them more obvious and unsightly. We have always dug a hole or trench for our toilet, out of sight of the tent area, on a site where the ground is soft and there is ample material to cover the job when finished.

We also prefer as much comfort as possible. One method is to select a biffy between two trees where a pair of poles can be lashed, one to sit on, the other as a back rest. At times, we have packed in a "toilet seat" sawed from a square of 1/4- inch plywood, built a pole frame over the hole and anchored the seat to the frame. We keep our roll of toilet paper within reach, stowed inside a lidded coffee can where it is safe from weather and from squirrels or chipmunks intent on chewing a hole through it. When abandoning camp, all poles are taken down and all holes, trenches or signs of bathroom activity concealed.

With the camp erected, fire site selected and biffy constructed, the next concern is drinking water. Over much of the northland, the lakes are generally considered clean enough to drink. But even in very remote areas this is not always the case. Our flat-tailed neighbors, the beavers, are carriers of a dreaded affliction called giardia, one that attacks human intestinal tracks and can create havoc with campers. We always boil the water we intend to drink at least 10 minutes to kill the bacteria. There are a number of water purification systems for campers that are also effective. Where fishing or hunting is done on a river downstream from any human habitation, it is best to carry the water along.

Campers today are often not aware that bedding at one time was a major concern. Blankets, sometimes held together with huge safety pins, were heavy, bulky and not particularly warm. Modern sleeping bags are comfortable, compact and designed for all types of weather. They only work, however, when dry and should be sealed up in plastic or packed in waterproof backpacks when traveling. Also, each camper gives off about one pint of water through breathing and perspiring every night. This water usually condenses and winds up inside the sleeping bag filling. It can reduce the bag's efficiency in a few nights if not dried out. In good weather, we hang our sleeping bags over a clothes line to air out while cooking breakfast. We hang them on a line under the kitchen tarp in wet weather.

Hunting camps present a more serious situation in that the heavier bags used are not as easily dried out. Two types of bags in common use are those stuffed with goose down and those stuffed with synthetic fiber. There is nothing warmer for the weight than goose down. But it can easily absorb moisture. In a cold weather camping situation, a good down bag may lose most of its insulation value in less than a week by absorbing moisture from the user. However, a combination of a synthetic fiber bag over a goose down liner will usually work well. Body moisture generated inside the bag tends to migrate as vapor outward, passing through the goose down and condensing in the synthetic fiber which is easier to dry out. This double bag system is one that works quite well even in extreme cold.

Another chronic sleeping bag problem is length. It pays to select a sleeping bag long enough to cover the entire body. A good rule of the thumb is to purchase a bag about 13 inches longer than the height of the camper. On cold nights, this will allow a person to slide down inside and stay cozy with maybe just the nose sticking out. Most bags today can be squoze into stuff bags. And the stuff bags can be filled with rolled up clothing at night to double as comfortable pillows.

For a good night's slumber, the mattress is just about as important as the bag. When we were kids, we just camped flat on the ground and thought nothing of it, but as age overtook us, we keep looking for more and more cushion beneath our weary bones. Luckily, modern campers have a wide variety of compact, lightweight camp mattresses available - foam pads, pads which can be inflated with air and pads which are a combination of both. All of these are designed to roll up into small packages when not in use. Some campers use only a "half pad," 42 to 48 inches long, just enough to accommodate their upper torsos with less concern for their legs. Others prefer full-length mats. Trial and error will usually make the final decision.

All campers need to carry flashlights, but for ordinary night illumination we prefer candles. Those thick "plumbers" candles burn longest and brightest. Some campers use a candle lantern which reflects the light. We simply anchor the candle on a flat rock and prop our metal shaving mirror behind it for reflected light. We save our flashlights for night trips to the biffy or other emergencies. Propane or gasoline lanterns can be useful in hunting camps where the hours of daylight are limited. However most of these lanterns emit toxic fumes and should be used mainly outside the tent.

No matter how careful a camper may be, sometimes damage will occur to the tent, sleeping bags or even the canoe. There is probably no more useful a product invented for camping than duct tape. We've used this stuff to patch holes in tent fabric, mosquito netting, rips in the rain fly and even holes in clothing. We have also used duct tape to cover some rather extensive damage to a canoe we once rolled up in a rapids we never should have attempted to run.

In extreme wet weather we take the kitchen tarp out of the duffle upon reaching a campsite. Before we do anything else, we rope out this 16x16 waterproof shelter, then bring up the packs and gear from the canoes. We erect our tent under the tarp, keeping it and our packs relatively dry. Similarly, if breaking camp in the rain, we pack up everything under the kitchen tarp, folding it up last. Once my wife and I traveled eight straight days in the rain using this method of keeping our gear dry. Although we got wet several times our gear didn't. We always had a fairly dry camp to sleep in under the kitchen fly.

On the last day, on our way home, the sun came out.

Chapter Seventeen
CHOW DOWN!

Ask any group of canoeists what the main hazards of a canoe trip are, and the list will include wind, rain, rapids or insects, but seldom the greatest threat of all: the activity which takes place at the cook fire. Almost any flatwater traveler can withstand howling winds, an occasional chilly spill and a host of gnawing creatures browsing on his dermis; but let him face a few meals with all the gustatory savor of rancid sheep mash and the trip goes up for grabs.

If more than two people are in the party, arbitration may reduce premeditated murder to simple verbal abuse. But there is really no need for any culinary confrontation, not with the variety of tasty, nutritious, lightweight, easy-to-prepare foods now available. Anyone who can read the instructions on the package can turn out a first class meal in 40 minutes. Not only has the trail food industry spawned a revolution in tasty meals but the shelves of super markets are jammed with all manner of foods requiring no more than water and heat for preparation.

The current generation of campers has landed in this trail food paradise without having passed through the purgatory of the old food wannigan packed with such staples as flour, beans, bacon and prunes, perhaps supplemented by 60 pounds of canned everything which consisted mainly of water. It was not just age that made the old time campers gnarled and stooped. It was the weight of the food packs.

Just a quick peek at the current list of available packaged items reveals omelets, blueberry pancakes, bacon-flavored scrambled eggs, creamed chicken, tuna with noodles, beef Stroganoff, shrimp creole, spaghetti and meatballs, coffee cake, chop suey, lasagna, turkey Tetrazzini, cheese Romanoff, chicken salad, fruit cobbler, apple compote, pineapple cheese cake, gelatin fruit salad, lemon pie, banana cream pie, and so on.

There are dozens of high-energy entrees that require no more than the addition of hot water. Freeze dried steaks or beef patties come out of the package looking like pressed cardboard, but dunked in hot water, they emerge as fresh products from the butcher's block. A few ounces of what appears to be confetti converts to carrots, peas, green beans, sweet corn or bell peppers.

Military surplus MRE's (Meals Ready to Eat) need only to be heated and eaten. There may be a few old hardheaded bush cooks who sneer at meals from packets; but history will probably assign these lard-stained old senior cooks to oblivion along with stage coach drivers and buffalo hunters. Not only can today's canoe chefs turn out tastier, better-balanced fare but with very little waste and spoilage. With better-preserved, bacteria-free packaged foods, there has been corresponding decrease in the incidence of intestinal disorders. From the standpoint of palate and stomach, these are truly the "good old days" of outdoor cookery.

None of this is intended to disparage experience with spoon and spatula. Even though a novice camp cook can turn out fair meals with today's ingredients, the veteran cook can create gourmet spreads through a knowledge of seasonings, timing and fresh additions from the waters and woodlands, bits of cook fire magic that come only with practice.

But first, forsooth, one must have a kitchen wherein to cook. Most outdoor cooks seek a fairly open spot, but sheltered from the wind. We like a fire site adjacent to a flat ledge where pots,

101

pans and food containers can be lined up as on a shelf. The grate may be adjusted horizontally by using a pan of water as a level and shim the low side of the grate with shards of rock. If wind becomes a problem, a few large, flat stones can be installed as a windbreak. If there is a hint of rain in the air, the kitchen fly may be slung at the rim of the fireplace sheltering the cooking and eating area. In no instance except extreme weather or if insect hordes are unbearable, is food taken inside the tent to eat. The attraction to bears is too great a risk.

There is nothing more handy than a table next to the fireplace and a flat bottom canoe upside down is an excellent substitute. We use two logs for supports at the bow and stern of the overturned canoe to provide steadiness. The canoe bottom will accommodate plates, cups, pots, utensils and food items. We also use the overturned canoe as a table when a camp stove is in use. With an aluminum canoe, we set the stove on top.

Every bush cook has his equipment preferences. There are serviceable aluminum cook kits made to accommodate from two to eight campers. We like the Mirro kits with a 12 inch frying pan for a lid. This pan is not much good for frying, but makes a fine mixing dish. We do most of our frying on a cast-aluminum griddle or a steel frying pan. And occasionally use a Dutch oven for baking. Some cooks prefer a reflector oven.

The cook kit is carried in a cloth bag with a draw string which helps

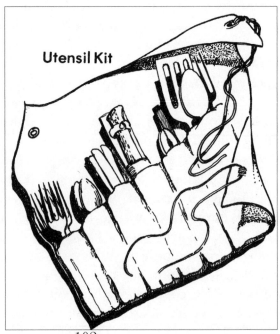

Utensil Kit

keep the kit separate from other items in the packsack. We also put the grate and griddle in separate cloth sacks. We make our own utensil bags, designed to hang on nearby trees, making knives, forks, spoons and cooking utensils handy. Like all north country guides, we carry long-nosed pliers in a sheath on our belt. The pliers are mainly for removing hooks from fish, but make excellent tongs for moving pots around on the fire.

Completing the cook tools are a sharp fillet knife, long-handled fork, spatula and a big spoon. A small, fine, flat file that fits in the utensil bag is excellent for sharpening. Some campers prefer whetstones. Take your pick.

We carry two types of fire starters in the pack: the GI-type tablets in foil which are used to kindle fires in wet situations and a roll of wax paper for general use. A small ball of bunched-up wax paper will start kindling quickly. Dry bark from dead and down birch trees is excellent fire starter when available.

A moderate stack of dry, foot-long "squaw wood," from the size of a pencil to thumb-thick, will provide enough easily regulated flame to cook anything. Where an open fire is used, we rub a layer of soap on the outsides of the pots. A dollop of liquid soap on a pot bottom can be spread by hand, taking care not to get any soap inside the pot. Smoky soot collects on the soap film which can be easily removed when washed, making pot cleaning less a chore than scrubbing the soot off with Brillo pads.

Before a match is struck, all food preparation that can be accomplished in advance is attended to in order to save time and fuel. At breakfast time this includes preparing orange juice. Two items we usually get heating first are the coffee pot and a pail of water which will be used for washing dishes. Coffee is brewed, not boiled, over a fire by putting one heaping tablespoon in coldwater for each four cups, plus a little extra "for the cook." The coffee is brought to a boil but is moved back from the flames but close enough so it continues to steep as the grounds settle.

If there is a diversity of beverage drinkers or if we are using a propane stove, water is heated to the boiling point then set aside to accommodate cups of instant coffee, tea, chocolate or bouillon. In cold weather we often make up cups of hot Tang - a superb frost dispeller.

The trick of putting together a fine shoreline meal is to get everything to be ready at the same time. Nobody likes to sit around watching fried fish get cold while the potatoes are cooking. Everything has a specific time to "get done" and thus the longest-cooking items are on first. Packaged foods have the cooking time printed thereon, which eliminates guesswork.

With a large group of anglers or hunters, it may not be possible to get everything on the fire at once. Bacon, for instance, can be cooked early, drained and set on paper inside a tin pan that can reflect the fire's heat while the pancakes or eggs are cooking.

Other dishes may be cooked in advance and set just off the fire to stay hot. Aluminum can quickly get too hot thus care must be taken not to get food charred inside a pot. Campers who curse black on the outside of a pot will need a whole new set of words to deal with black inside a pot. One way to control a fire's heat is to periodically flip a few spoons of water on the flames.

There are some food items which have withstood the test of a time and are as good as 100 years ago, such as bannock. This is pan bread which can be baked ahead of time or prepackaged as dry ingredients and baked on the trail. Wrapped in foil or plastic, bannock will keep for days on end and goes with just about any meal.

It is made thus: Starting with three cups of flour, add together a tablespoon of baking powder, a little sugar, half a teaspoon of salt, a double handful of raisins or cut up dried fruit and a half cup of dried milk. After mixing well, add two tablespoons of cooking oil and a cup of water, slowly kneading the dough until it turns into a rubbery ball. Dust a little flour on the canoe "table" and punch the rubber dough into flat disc the same size as the bottom of the frying pan. Grease the pan, drop in the dough and let the pan sit on the fire until the dough begins to brown on the bottom. Take the pan off and prop it up with rocks facing the fire, about a foot away and allow the top to bake until it begins to brown. It is ready to eat then or can be stowed away for later.

We do not take meat, other than bacon, along on any fishing or hunting trips because there are tons of fish under our canoe and there is abundant wild game in the nearby forests and marshes. On a fishing trip, we eat fish every day - fried, poached, baked, broiled or made into chowder. One easy way to fix fish is to cut off the heads, pull out the entrails and cut the carcass up the back so it is held together by the belly section. Salted and simply laid on the fire grate, scale side down, it can be broiled. A strip of bacon or a dab of oil on a fish fillet may add flavor. Fish cook quickly this way and can be eaten right out of the skin.

Pike are found abundantly over the northern canoe country, but some people hesitate to eat them because of the bones. Boning pike filets is not difficult and can be accomplished thus:

Cut each fillet into three-inch pieces. The tail section has no bones and may be set aside. The other pieces have the tips of the "Y" bones protruding slightly on the inside near the lateral line. A thumb run along the lateral line will detect them. This is the top of the "Y." The tail curves below and toward the dorsal. Insert the knife above the top of the "Y," cut down and out toward the dorsal. This removes a slice of boneless meat. The next cut is made behind the lower part of the "Y" bones taking out the bones to be discarded. The remainder is bone-free. With practice a pike can be boned in a jiffy and provides excellent ingredients for a fish dinner, among them Finnish mojakka.

Finnish what? The dish is pronounced moy-yahka. It is a type of chowder and is made thus: Several onions are cut up and heated in oil on the bottom of a large pot until they become transparent. Pike (or any other fish) are cut into one-inch pieces and added as a layer over the onions. Over the fish is placed a layer of cut up potatoes. Follow with other layers of fish and potatoes until all the ingredients are used up. Each layer is lightly salted and peppered as added. Fill the pot with enough water to just cover the last layer of potatoes. Bring it to a boil. A golf ball size bag of pickling spice is hung into the pot on a string. The heat is cut back and the pot simmered for one hour. At that point, the pickling spice is removed, a can of condensed milk or packet of powdered milk and a quarter of butter or margarine is gently stirred into the pot. It is now ready. Stand back!

Fish remains can be left on shore rocks some distance from the camp where seagulls will dispose of them.

In season, we make use of wild berries, particularly blueberries which are found in copious amounts. These can be added to cereal, put in pancake batter, added to muffins and added to darn near anything to enhance the flavor.

On hunting trips, we roast grouse or wild duck over the coals, usually wrapped in foil with a couple of bacon and onion strips laid on the breast to add flavor. On deer hunting expeditions by canoe, we dress out the first deer taken, cook the liver and heart plus a portion of the tenderloin. We often cut up a section of shoulder for hunter's stew.

Canoe paddling bums up a lot of calories. To keep the paddlers interior furnace stoked, a handful or two of gorp, candy, dried fruit or other munchies helps maintain energy between meals. At least once every hour we stop for a drink of water, a necessity to prevent dehydration.

Chapter Eighteen
BEWARE THE WENDIGO

Our more or less Christian forbearers, by dint of considerable effort and courage, managed to settle this great north country, but not without controversy involving the native inhabitants. This controversy sometimes spilled over into warfare and even after peace treaties, continues in courts of law to this day. In a very real sense, we are fishing and hunting by canoe in the tribal waters of Ojibwe canoemen, using their concepts and their design of watercraft.

In many respects, such as canoe materials, camping equipment, fishing tackle and firearms, we have improved considerably on the native gear. But there are some things we might ponder as we pursue our sports on what were once tribal waters: One is that the American Indian had a very close relationship with his environment, its fish and wildlife. And he had a working relationship and great respect for the various spirits he believed dwelt hereabouts.

Those of us who were born to immigrant families coming from Europe are known by the Ojibwe people as "ch-mooka-mon" or "long knives." Some of the earliest white travelers were soldiers, men with swords and bayonets. We "ch-mooka-mon" brought our own culture and belief in God with us. And, to some degree, a rather condescending attitude toward the native beliefs in spirits of the forests and waters, spirits which are mainly labeled as "superstition."

Yet, it is difficult to find a single old time guide or veteran paddler of the northern canoe trails, who does not accept to greater or lesser extent, some of the native beliefs in forces beyond our control. Some say they have witnessed what appear to be sorry results of disbelief. Some say they have met one or more of those native spirits face to face and thus advise softly: "Scoff at your own peril."

The Ojibwe believe there are spirits both friendly and baleful and it may not be easy to recognize which ones a person might perhaps encounter. Woven into the Ojibwe culture is a belief in Naniboujou, a trickster who delights in changing into other forms such as a rabbit, and whom engages in deceit as well as benevolence. He may provide fish when one is hungry, but he may also tip the coffee pot over causing scalding liquid to sear one's hand or he may nudge one's arm to cause the fillet knife to take a slice out of a thumb. A couple of times we have suspected that Naniboujou, in a fit of perversity, altered a backcast to follow an errant course causing the hooks of a fishing lure to become embedded in someone's scalp. We have also sensed that Naniboujou, while in the form of a fish, suddenly thrashed about in the bottom of a canoe and buried a hook in an angler's hand. For these episodes, white men blame each other or the fish. The Native Folk blame Naniboujou.

The Ojibwe forest, "meh-gway-ahk," is home, they believe, to numerous tiny beings called Maymay-guish. These invisible, diminutive creatures delight in stealing or misplacing things. Who has not filleted a catch of walleyes, carried the fillets up to the fire place for cooking and returned to the shore only to find the fillet knife is now missing? The rock where the fish were cleaned is there, but the knife is mysteriously vanished.

Sometime later the knife turns up, but at another place on the shore. How could that be? The Ojibwe believe the May-may-guish moved it. They also delight in stealing the container of matches or shaker of salt. They create no end of irritating problems around a

108

camp; but once their presence is recognized, steps may be taken to foil at least some of their efforts. The Indians insist nobody will ever see one, but they point out that in the evening, as the sun is setting and we sit by the dying fire, if we listen carefully, we may hear the Maymay-guish laughing in the treetops. "It is just an evening breeze," the skeptic may say. Old timers and Ojibwe people know differently.

But these are funny beings. Not so funny are the evil spirits. One of these is Missabishew, the water lynx. As one travels through the North American canoe country, pictographs - ancient paintings on the rocks - may be viewed in a number of places. These native paintings, rendered with iron oxide in fish oil centuries ago, show people in canoes, cranes, wolves, moose and other animals ... and also Missabishew. This lizardlike creature has legs, a long tail and horns on its head. The Ojibwe believe it dwells at the base of huge cliffs and in watery caves. When they pass by these haunts, they leave offerings of tobacco - the sacred ah-say-mah - stuffed in cracks to appease the wrathful lynx. Failure to do so invites the risk of having a sudden windstorm arise and overturn the canoe with dire results.

And then there is the Wendigo, most dreaded of all. Directly translated from the Ojibwe language, a Wendigo is a cannibal. In ancient times, when Indian families lived in isolation on the hunting grounds for entire winters, sometimes food supplies ran out. Thus it was that scouts or hunters would occasionally come across a camp where there was no one left except perhaps one or two gaunt, deranged figures dwelling among the bones of what were formerly family members or neighbors.

Wendigos were always shunned and looked upon with fear. These malevolent spirits are believed to never die, but wander forever seeking victims. The Ojibwe believe there is a Wendigo dwelling in every waterfall and every set of dangerous rapids. This concept may have originated from the fact that in some cases where a native canoeman swamped in roaring rapids, his body was tumbled around among the rocks and sometimes emerged with an arm or leg missing. The Wendigo ripped it off, they believe.

109

Perhaps.

Learned white men have written books about native beliefs and superstitions, perhaps attempting to interpret these beliefs from a white man's perspective or in relation to modem psychological knowledge; but those of us who have paddled the canoe routes for many decades have experienced things not explained in the libraries of science or in the cultural background of the white man's world. When we travel through native tribal lands and on their waters we take care to follow the native ways. Their beliefs become our beliefs. Where they put out a tobacco offering, we put out a tobacco offering. We take no chances.

However, no matter how careful or observant one may be, sometimes painful accidents or sickness may occur on a fishing or hunting canoe trip. If it happens in wilderness country, some distance from medical help, it behooves the traveler to have a functional first aid kit along and the knowledge of how to use it.

For many years, a number of us who live on the rim of the federal Boundary Waters Canoe Area Wilderness served with various search and rescue units locating and retrieving the injured, the sick and, occasionally, the dead. We were on 24-hour standby, ready to go at a moment's notice, summer or winter. Our efforts were coordinated by mobile radio with the Boy Scout National High Adventure Base on Moose Lake, the Lake County Sheriffs Department, Minnesota State Conservation Officers, floatplane operators and the local clinic and hospital. In later years, this work has been taken over entirely by trained search and rescue teams from northern sheriffs departments and the DNR, but the need for first aid knowledge has never diminished.

There are annually a number of very good first aid courses offered in most communities, either through the Red Cross or by medical staff members from clinics or hospitals. The skills gained are invaluable and the knowledge of applying first aid makes it possible for each person to make up an appropriate medical kit.

Of particular concern are people afflicted with insect or other allergies and with chronic medical problems such as diabetes. Because there are now medicines to control these afflictions, individuals may continue to enjoy the canoe trails, but only if they remember to pack their medications. We have known a number of diabetic paddlers who enjoyed fishing, hunting and canoeing just like anyone else. There are outdoor folk with cardiac problems, but with their medication they get along quite well.

However, unforeseen accidents may occur and it is best to be prepared. Cuts, minor or major, may happen and require treatment to prevent infection. If an injury is very serious, first aid may be administered before the victim is brought out to a medical facility. Bandaids of various sizes, large and small, butterfly closures, a roll of one-inch and two-inch cotton bandage, several large gauze pads, rolls of Dermicel tape or something similar, several Telfa pads, 2-inch and 3-inch Coban bandages, several tongue depressors, scissors, tweezers, scalpel, a single edge razor blade, germicidal soap, antibacterial ointment, several large safety pins, aspirin, laxative, extra waterproofed kitchen matches and a small note pad and pencil are good enough for starters.

The pad and pencil are for emergencies where the victim cannot be safely moved by canoe and outside help is required. The victim's name, address, detailed location and believed trauma are written down and sent out with members of the canoe group going to seek help, or given to anyone passing by. The exact location of the victim may be pinpointed on a map for delivery to rescue personnel. If it is possible to call 911 on a cell phone, relating the exact location of the victim will insure speedy help from float plane pilots or ground rescue people.

Every canoeist should be familiar with signals used to mark accident sites. Three fires sending up three columns of smoke are standard. Three T-shirts on tree limbs, three of anything in tandem indicate trouble. Blaze orange tarps or tent flies laid out on shoreline rocks can be spotted easily from the air. Crossed paddles laid on a tarp or rock indicate trouble. A person standing on a lake shore waving a paddle or T-shirt on a stick can be spotted from a considerable distance. Emergency flares, the type carried by motorists, can be seen from a considerable distance.

Long-nosed pliers, used to remove hooks from fish, are also

handy for removing hooks from people. Instead of carrying a small pocket handkerchief, some canoeists carry a large bandanna which can double as a sling in an emergency. A sharp pocket knife and a length of eighth-inch nylon line can be useful in making and applying splints to sprains or breaks.

Every individual doesn't need a first aid kit, but one for the group is essential. Also, anyone with allergies or other individual medical problems, should inform others in the group so that if an emergency occurs, someone other than the victim can identify the problem and deal with it.

Medical people advise anglers and hunters to have current tetanus shots. It is true that tetanus or "lockjaw" can be gotten from a cut on something rusty, but it can happen just as easy with a cut from a knife, sharp rock or protruding branch. The bacillus that causes tetanus lives in the ground and in animal feces. It can be encountered anywhere dirt gets into a wound. Tetanus shots are inexpensive and easy to obtain. Everyone's family doctor should have a record of such shots so that immunization can be kept current.

In most canoe books, reference is made to hypothermia, a condition caused by a drop in body temperature. Lowering body temperature just a few degrees may cause severe chills, chattering teeth, numbness slurred speech, hallucinations and convulsions leading to death. Of particular concern is falling into cold water or being beset by cold rain and wind. Anglers in the spring have such concerns. Similarly with hunters in the fall when lakes are cold. Cold, windy rain can allow hypothermia to sneak up on unsuspecting paddlers intent upon pursuing their sport.

What occurs when body temperature begins to decline is an uncontrolled reaction in which the body heat is concentrated around the vital organs - the heart and lungs. The body automatically slows circulation to the extremities, including the head. The individual has absolutely no control over this phenomenon. First symptoms, other than shivering, are slurred speech, apathy, fumbling, stumbling and lack of coordination.

To counter this, warm drinks may be administered. The victim

112

can be wrapped in a dry sleeping bag (in an extreme case, a healthy individual can also crawl into the bag to provide additional heat.) A fire may be kindled and the victim placed where heat can be absorbed.

However, prevention is best. Most fishermen and hunters, swamping in cold water, recognize that they need to get out of the water immediately and get a fire going. External heat supplemented by hot drinks will prevent problems from arising. Less understood and more subtle is the threat from cold rain and wind. Paddlers driving into a rain storm, may feel relatively warm, but may still become afflicted by slowly lowered body temperature. The fact that the outside temperature is not below freezing can be deceptive. Individuals who get wet in a windy situation are at considerable risk. The problem is that once hypothermia begins, the lack of warm blood flowing to the brain creates the deception that things are going just fine. The victim of hypothermia has no way of knowing how bad things have become.

Thus it is essential that the angler or hunter be aware of a potential hypothermic situation before it can occur. Wet. Cold. Wind. These are key words. Experienced canoemen pay attention and avoid trouble. They stay safe, dry and warm.

Earlier in this chapter, reference was made to various Ojibwe spirits and the advisability of heeding the native beliefs. The Ojibwe people have a saying: "The white man is a slow learner." And many of us come to a more or less better understanding of such matters only through trial and error.

Once, many moons ago, when my wife and I were quite young, we were making a motion picture of a canoe fishing trip on the border waters between the U.S. and Canada. We had filmed extensive footage of catching fish, cooking fish, pitching camp, paddling and portaging, but felt we needed something unusual, something exciting to finish out the movie.

In late afternoon, we were coming east up Iron Lake, approaching Curtain Falls, the 35-foot cascade at the outlet of Crooked Lake. A slanting sun cast a soft, orange glow on the curtain of mist surrounding the falls, creating a spectacular scene. At the base of the falls lies a large slick pool which empties in a rush of foam and a short, steep chute and into a series of rapids flowing into Iron Lake. The lower three rapids we had negotiated a number of times before, but there was a well-worn portage around the upper one and around the falls.

Sizing up the situation, we determined that a segment of whitewater action would spice up the show. My wife set up the camera on a ledge at the top of the first rapids while I intended to push off alone in the canoe, cross the pool and go sailing down the rapids in a shower of foam and glory. As I proceeded to the shore, preparing to enter the pool below the falls. I was startled when a familiar voice at my elbow inquired: "What are you doing, Bob?"

It was an old Indian friend, Stanley Owl, who was portaging upstream to Crooked Lake and happened to be passing by. "I'm going to paddle around the base of the falls," I said to Stanley. "And then run my canoe through that first rapids while my wife gets it all on film."

Stanley looked at me soberly. "You can't do that," he warned.

"Whatta you mean?"

"There's a Wendigo in that rapids," Stanley said. "Tried it once with another canoeman and we smashed up ... both of us ended up in the hospital. Almost got killed by that Wendigo."

"A Wendigo?" I laughed. "You don't believe that old superstitious stuff, do you Stanley?"

He stared at me and shook his head. "You can't go in there."

At that point in my life I was invincible, immortal and absolutely sure of my own ability. "You just watch me, Stanley," I assured him.

Thereupon I pushed off, paddled past the base of the falls, crossed the pool and headed for the rapids and the camera. To this day I think I could have made it if a gust of wind or something hadn't sluiced the canoe six feet sideways. At the last moment, the canoe jumped sideways, missed the center of the chute, shot over a rock ledge at the side and plunged nose-first into the suds. I jammed my head forward under the center thwart and grabbed the gunwales as the canoe cracked into the bottom rocks.

114

The canoe was an old time aluminum model with air compartments fore and aft As the bow smashed bottom, the front was ripped and all forward floatation vanished - which I was not aware of at the time. The underside of the rapids churned like a huge automatic washer, a maelstrom of suds, whirling the canoe and me, banging and bumping over huge boulders like something had us in a fierce grip and wouldn't let go. A force grabbed at my pants and tore both knees out, then ripped the front of my shirt. There was a sound like something was chewing the whole front of the canoe to tinfoil.

Somehow, I managed to break free of the wreck, popped to the surface and gulped in some air. The wrecked canoe went bumping down another set of rapids while I struck out for the closest shore which happened to be on the opposite side of the river. Waterlogged and battered, I managed to crawl up on the bank in time to see Stanley push off his canoe to come across and pick me up.

"There is something in that rapids," I gasped through chattering teeth as he paddled up. "It had me in its grip but I got lucky and managed to get away." Stanley stared at me deadpanned with his hard, black eyes. He didn't say a word.

A Wendigo? I'm glad I didn't find out.

Chapter Nineteen
WHEN THE HUNTER BECOMES THE HUNTED

All canoeists believe, sometimes correctly, that there are things in the outdoors that can "getcha."

First that comes to mind among some paddlers is an attack from a bear. Fortunately, other than the grizzly, bears are not particularly antisocial. The black bear is a somewhat calm, non-aggressive species, at least so far as humans are concerned, although it can create problems in regard to food packs. The black bear is also an accomplished actor and is known to put on a fierce face and emit growling threats in attempts to create fear in the heart of a camper. But they seldom do anything dangerous, with one exception, and that is if the bear is attacked. Two instances we know about were initiated by aggressive people. One was a man who went after a bear that had his food pack. The camper kicked the bear in the ribs, attempting to make it release the pack. The bear struck back, knocking the camper to the ground and leaving some claw marks in his leg.

The second occurred when a friend of ours was attempting to close his resort for winter. A bear got into an altercation with our friend's Labrador retriever, indeed, had it by the head. Our friend ran up and booted the bear in the face which caused the bear to drop the dog and go after his attacker, knocking him down and batting him around the knees before breaking off hostilities. Our friend required several stitches to close the gashes in his knees.

The grizzly is an altogether different breed and is apt to take umbrage with any trespassers. However, unless a person is paddling in grizzly country, this is no problem. Indeed, the real or imaginary hazards of the canoe country are an insignificant fraction of the danger involved with driving up and driving home on the highway. Traffic is a lot deadlier than anything on the canoe routes.

In all the national parks there are signs reading: "Do not feed the wildlife." This is sage advice. However, it is often impossible to avoid feeding some, particularly those smaller predators like black flies and mosquitoes. Of the two, mosquitoes are easier to deal with because they are literate. That is, if a bottle of insect repellant carries the message on its label: "Repels mosquitoes," it very likely will. However, if it says: "Repels all noxious insects," it very likely has no effect on black flies. Most wilderness guides are therefore of the opinion that black flies are illiterate and cannot read the labels.

At one point in the history of man vs. bug, there was an elixir bottled by LJB Laboratories in St. John, Michigan, called BF 100. It did repel black flies rather effectively. However, the federal EPA determined that there were chemicals in BF 100 which were also not good for humans, and outlawed it.

Repellents with Deet, which works on some bugs, doesn't much deter black flies. An alternative is to peg pants cuffs into wool sox, wear shirts with long sleeves and don a head net. Otherwise, slap. Black flies not only create an itchy lump at the point of contact, but secrete a venom which can cause listlessness and nausea. People allergic to insects may experience swelling of arms, legs or faces. Those of us who live in black fly country, usually develop some-

117

what of an immunity to the venom over a course of years, but not entirely.

Mosquitoes, on the other hand, are not particularly benign. One may ponder how the Native People and the French Voyageurs made it through the wilderness without effective repellants or head nets. They had only the wind in the daytime and perhaps a smoky fire at night to repel them.

Bites are just part of the problem. A mosquito in the tent at night is an immediate source of irritation. It is difficult to fall asleep with one of these miniature vampires whining in the dark. One effective procedure is to call an air raid alert, going on the offensive with a flashlight in one hand and an aerosol bomb in the other. Since quite lethal, the fumes from the spray are not recommended for humans to inhale. Some campers give their tent a shot or two of insecticide an hour or so before a turning in. This not only kills any bugs in the tent but allows the chemicals to disperse.

Other small pests are ordinary houseflies, chiggers and noseeums. All of these can usually be warded off with repellant. While bees, hornets and wasps can all be problems, they are visible and can be avoided. Wasp nests - round, paper-like bags hanging from branches - are items to be let alone. Luckily there are nostrums which alleviate the sting and itch of bug bites and may be included in the first aid kit.

Ticks are constantly with us. The common wood tick is a persistent vampire which not only removes blood but leaves a swelling, itching wound. Deer ticks are small, usually reddish, and are carriers of Lyme disease, a debilitating affliction. Ticks may be removed with a tweezers. The wound of a deer tick may be indicated by a round, reddish ring around the bite area. Any such affliction should be promptly checked by a doctor. There is treatment for Lyme disease if caught in the early stages.

So much for bugs. Back to mammals. The black bear, although somewhat of a threat in mythology, is mainly a problem of food packs. Packs left within reach of these raiders is fair game and a lot of canoe trips are ended prematurely each summer due to stolen food. Grub packs may be hoisted into the air, out of bear's reach, by using a rope over a tree limb. The pack cannot be slung within reach of the tree trunk, however, or bruin will have it. Some campers use a rope between two trees to put the food out of reach. Other campers prefer the new, airtight metal food canisters, which do not seem to be bothered by bears even when sitting out on a campsite. The belief is that the airtight design contains the odor of food. We do not know of any instances where bears bothered food in these airtight containers.

Worst case scenario is food brought inside a tent. This is a definite invitation to a hungry bear. Sometimes, simply out of curiosity, a bear will invade a camp when the occupants are out fishing. If the tent is zipped up and if there is the odor of food emanating from within, the bear will likely create a new door and probably a new exit when he leaves. We have always left our tents open and unzipped during the day. Bears wishing to visit will usually walk in, look around and walk out. Some guides we know pack along an extra, half-used bug bomb as a bear deterrent. If a bear is sighted near camp, a strip of bacon is wrapped around the bug bomb and tied on securely with fish line. This booby trap is left near the fireplace where it will be quickly located by a raiding bear. He will first try to lick the bacon loose and failing that, will bite through both bacon and aerosol can.. The resulting explosion usually clears the bear's sinuses and also clears him out of the campsite.

Bears sometimes exhibit bizarre behavior. Once we outfitted a honeymoon couple that set up camp on an island they felt was beyond a bear's reach. Not so. The first morning at breakfast time, a bear swam over to the island, then made a dash through the camp like a football running back, scooped up a Duluth pack, tucked it under one arm and bolted for the woods. Whether the newlyweds or the bear were more surprised is open to debate because that packsack contained only clothing. When the couple regained their composure, they cautiously followed the path taken by the bear. Strewn along the path were shirts, pants, sox and underwear and eventually the empty pack tossed aside by the frustrated bear.

Guide Harry Lambirth was once camped on an island in Ensign

Lake and observed a huge bear making a raid on an adjacent island. The campers were out fishing and had taken the precaution of roping their food pack high off the ground. The baffled bruin marched back and forth apparently getting angrier by the minute. Unable to reach the pack, he let out a bellow of disgust, turned and stamped the tent flat. He didn't just knock it down, he stomped on it. This is the only incident of that type we ever heard of.

Some guides rate moose as the only genuinely dangerous critter in the north woods and then only during the rut in October. We have known of occasions where anglers were harassed by an angry bull and this is not anything amusing. One fall, bush pilot Kenny Bellows was coming across the 700-yard portage from Disappointment Lake to Snowbank Lake and was chased by a bull. Kenny dropped his stringer of fish, shinnied up a tree and looked down. The bull stamped, stormed and banged the tree trunk with his antlers before stalking back into the woods. Kenny climbed back down, but went right back up as the bull came charging back. It had apparently just moved out of sight, waiting to see what Kenny would do. Kenny remained in the tree for over an hour with no sign nor sound of the moose. Eventually, he eased back down to the ground, grabbed his stringer of fish and took off at a fast sprint for the boat. In seconds, he was backing the outboard away from shore and headed for home. The moose made no further appearance.

Once, fishing on a stream near Mercutio Lake in Ontario, my wife and I surprised a moose calf that tried to get out of our way but got its back legs hung up over a streamside sapling. We watched with interest as it struggled and bawled, but then began paddling furiously away when the cow moose came thundering out of the woods in a high state of motherly anger.

Over all the northern canoe country, there are no poisonous snakes; but not so in the south. Both moccasins and rattlers may be found streamside and have been known to drop off a limb into a canoe. Once my friend George Arthur and I were float fishing on Missouri's Current River, taking turns with one of us casting from the bow and the other handling the canoe from the stern. It was my turn on the paddle and as we approached a deep pool, I eased the canoe alongside a large, downed oak and grabbed the bark to hold the canoe in place while George made few casts. A movement next to my arm brought me quickly alert. About 18 inches from my left elbow lay the thick body and beady-eyed head of a moccasin, studying me with obvious distaste. The snake and I stared at each other briefly; then I carefully released my grip and let the canoe drift away. While I have seen a lot of snakes on canoe trips, this was the only poisonous one that was threatening. Canoeists who travel snake country usually pack along an anti-venom kit, just in case.

Rodents can be a problem. Squirrels and chipmunks have a bad habit of entering packs and chewing into boxes or packets of food. They also have a thing about boring holes into toilet paper rolls. Skunks can be a hazard to hunting dogs. A retriever or a bird dog that challenges a skunk is apt to be unwelcome back in a canoe. About all that can be done at the time is to take the dog to the shore and scrub it down with dish soap. Washing a dog in tomato juice will usually remove skunk odor, but few canoeists carry a can of tomato juice along.

Mice, on some well-used campsites, may attempt to invade food packs. Also, they sometimes engage in strange antics at night. One autumn when my wife and I were camped on Fourtown Lake we were awakened sometime around midnight by a company of little deer mice which repeatedly climbed up to the tent peak and slid down the tent fly, trip after trip. Eventually, we shook the tent fly and they left.

Porcupines are rather indolent creatures that seldom pose a threat to people, but are a definite hazard to dogs. Several times we have been involved with dogs that attempted to bite a porky and wound up with a face full of painful quills. It usually takes two or more persons to remove the quills - one to hold the dog securely while the other pulls out the darts with pliers. It is no fun for anyone, particularly the dog.

These are some of the hazards which may occur with various forms of wildlife, but few on the canoe trails are ever life-threatening. As noted before, the highway is much more dangerous than the canoe country, not only with traffic, but also with such mammals as deer and moose. In our home state of Minnesota, some 16,000 deer-car collisions are recorded each year and several dozen moose-car accidents. Many of these involve serious injury, even death to the motorists and almost always death to the animal. When driving through the North American canoe country, particularly at night, it pays to be extra alert to creatures on the road or in the ditches along the road.

Chapter 20
TIME TO MAKE CAMP

My friend, we have traveled some distance together. Perhaps we have managed to exchange some ideas on fishing and hunting from a canoe which could be of some use.

Let it be understood that this is not the final word on the subject. There will never be a final word on the subject because new ideas and new equipment continually evolves. The author has over 80 years of canoe experience and has enjoyed every moment of it. Like the Native American paddlers, this old courier du bois recognizes that in the great scheme of things, time eventually runs out for all species, including man.

The Ojibwe canoemen have a belief called "Be-mah-di-zee-win." It is the "Circle of Life" where all living things dwell in this circle - the fish the game, the birds and even people. In their understanding of life, all creatures are equal. All have a time to be born, a time to live and a time to die. That understanding has served the Ojibwe well and perhaps it is something to consider by all who travel the tribal waterways.

For me, it has been a remarkable eight decades on the water and I give thanks to the Great Spirit for allowing me to participate. Like the Ojibwe, I recognize that somewhere toward the setting sun "nee-gah-be-ee-noong" lies Spirit Land where the fish and game are plentiful, the sun always shines, the days are ever warm and the wind is gentle on the water.

If you come that way some day and see my camp, paddle over and pull up your canoe. The coffee pot will be on the fire.